NEGRO SLAVERY
IN LATIN AMERICA

NEGRO SLAVERY IN LATIN AMERICA

Rolando Mellafe

translated by J. W. S. Judge

UNIVERSITY OF CALIFORNIA PRESS

BERKELEY   LOS ANGELES   LONDON

University of California Press
Berkeley and Los Angeles, California

University of California Press, Ltd.
London, England

Copyright © 1975, by
The Regents of the University of California

ISBN 0-520-02106-1
Library of Congress Catalog Card Number: 78-170720
Printed in the United States of America

TO MARIA TERESA, ALEJANDRA,
AND CAROLINA

CONTENTS

INTRODUCTION

Latin America is a combination of racial groups that vary in degree of integration in each of the different republics. Some countries are highly homogeneous, others more or less integrated, while a number are markedly differentiated according to color variations which approximately correspond to the range of social and economic status. Given such circumstances, the institutional, economic, and social implications of more than three centuries of Negro slavery cannot be other than pertinent. The forms that slavery took in Latin America, the extent of its development in the various regions, and the specific ways in which it came to an end, are all basic to a clearer understanding of Latin America and its culture. This study is intended to give an idea of the problem first by the briefest possible summary of its historical development, and second by the inclusion of a relatively full, though select, bibliography.

The institution of Negro slavery, because of related social and economic issues, gave rise to a voluminous mass of archival source material in both America and Europe. Some of the archival sources have been included in the bibliography. Besides documentary material of this nature, many people, beginning with those on Columbus' first voyage, have written on the subject with differing interests and aims. In this Introduction I shall refer to the most important works, from a historical point of view, written in both the Old and the New World. The first to deal with Negro slavery in America was the *Historia de las Indias* of Fray Bartolomé

1

de las Casas.[1] He was also the first person to question, in fiery condemnation, the legitimacy of the methods of European colonization in America. He was primarily interested in the Indians, and it was because of both their rapidly dwindling numbers in the Antilles and their weakened position as a labor force on the mainland that Negro slavery was brought to America.

Immediately after Las Casas, however, attention became almost exclusively centered on the practical problems of productivity and shortage of labor. Slavery was taken completely for granted as an ancient tradition with its roots in classical and medieval times. The local town councils, regional high courts, governors, administrators, representatives of the crown, writers, thinkers, and historians of the times all referred in one way or another to African slaves, generally with the motive of increasing the supply of slaves or of seeking a reduction or removal of the customs duties and taxes to which the slave trade was subject. These are points that will also be taken up in the text. Here, as a good example among the mass of available documents and books, one may cite the two petitions made by Antonio de León Pinelo, one of the best-known treatise writers and jurists of the seventeenth century. He presented his petitions to the king in 1623 and 1624, and in them he strongly urged the importation of more slaves on behalf of several colonial towns of the time.[2]

[1] Las Casas (1474-1566): The *Historia* was begun in 1527 and completed in 1561, but it was not until 1875-76 that the manuscript was published by the *Real Academia*. Las Casas has been variously called the "Apostle" or "Protector of the Indians," as well as denigratory names as the result of his policies and the ways by which he advanced them. Undoubtedly his major contribution to the betterment of the lot of native peoples lay at court rather than in his work in the Indies. He unceasingly attacked the forced labor of Indians either by enslavement or as the de facto result of granting allotments of Indian labor to leading settlers (the *encomienda* system), albeit the object of the latter, in theory, was to Christianize and "protect" them in return for the right to exact labor and payment of tribute. Las Casas is regarded as largely responsible for the enactment of the New Laws of 1542-1543, which attempted to suppress the encomienda system gradually and to eliminate Indian slavery. See Henry R. Wagner and Helen R. Parish, *The Life and Writings of Bartolomé de las Casas* (Albuquerque, 1967) (for the New Laws, see pp. 108-120); Lewis Hanke, *The Spanish Struggle for Justice in the Conquest of America* (Philadelphia, 1949); and also Hanke's Introduction to the *Historia* (see Section 2 of Bibliography, under Las Casas, 1951).

[2] See Bibliography. The 1623 petition, for example, was made to Philip IV "on

A very important work was the *De Instauranda Aeth-iopum Salute* by Alonso de Sandoval published in 1627. It was written at the height of the trade in Cartagena, one of the major slaving ports on the Caribbean coast of Colombia. One of Sandoval's leading disciples was St. Peter Claver, who became known as the "Saint of the Slaves" in Latin America. Besides dealing with the problem of the evangelization of recently arrived Negroes, Sandoval attempted to investigate their African tribal origins and customs, their artistic inter-ests, and their forms of social organization. Perhaps without explicitly intending to do so, he left to posterity one of the most significant ethnographic studies of black culture now available.[3]

In the eighteenth century, the change of dynasty in Spain, its attendant political struggles and wars, the attempts at economic recuperation, and the new ideological principles of the Age of Enlightenment gave rise to a huge quantity of books, petitions, and opinions on Negro slavery. Included were such works as the *Voto consultivo* by Pedro Bravo de Lagunas; the *Representación de los hacendados* by Mariano Moreno; and the heavy, erudite articles, typical of the eighteenth century, which appeared in *El Mercurio Peruano* of Lima between 1791 and 1795.[4]

Except in a few cases where there was contemporary

---

behalf of the imperial seat of Potosí, of the City of La Serena, the Kingdom of Chile . . . , for permission and license for entry . . . of slaves from Guinea."

[3] See Bibliography. Sandoval: 1576 (Spain)-1652 (Cartagena). He went to Peru with his family when still very young. There he entered the Jesuit order and was in due course sent to Cartagena. An earlier, lesser-known work with similar preoccupations, and also basic to a knowledge of African slaves, was his *Naturaleza sagrada y profana, costumbres, ritos y supersticiones de todos los Etíopes* (1627). His *De Instauranda Aethiopum Salute* was published in 1641. By his reference to Ethiopians he simply means Negroes.

St. Peter Claver: 1580 (Spain)-1654 (Cartagena). He was sent by the Jesuits in 1610 to Cartagena, where he met Sandoval. He was very much concerned with the conditions in which the slaves arrived. He was canonized in 1888.

[4] The last of the Spanish Hapsburgs was Charles II (1665-1700), who named Philip, Duke of Anjou of the French house of Bourbon, to succeed him. The latter's coming to the throne as Philip V (1700-1746) brought about a period of greater French influence in Spain and the War of the Spanish Succession (1701-1713).

For Bravo de Lagunas, see Bibliography. For Mariano Moreno, see under Diego Luis Molinari, 1939, in Section 2 of the Bibliography. See also *Idea de las congrega-ciones publicas de los negros bozales* in the "Biblioteca Peruana de Historia," vol. VIII, Lima, 1864. How far the principles and writings of the Enlightenment had practical results will be considered in the text.

interest in presenting accounts of events occurring in the colonies, many years were to elapse before interest in Latin America would cease to concentrate on the exclusively pragmatic aspects of the political and economic circumstances of slavery, and turn to the more analytic approaches of the social sciences. It was no coincidence that when the change came it occurred in two of the countries where slavery was most important and where it lasted the longest—Cuba and Brazil. In Cuba the attractive polemic nature of Antonio José Saco (1797-1879) produced the first contemporary historical study of the institution of slavery. It was his *Historia de la escalvitud desde los tiempos más remotos hasta nuestros días*, published posthumously in Havana in 1893, that traced the general history of slavery from the earliest times. He had spent some 30 years on research in order to write the work. It is still fundamental. Approximately a third of it comprises a complete coverage of slavery in Latin America.[5] While Saco's work was being published in Cuba, in Salvador da Bahia the eminent Brazilian, Raimundo Nina Rodrigues, was beginning a series of studies on African cultures in both their place of origin and in the New World within a context of cultural contribution and interchange.[6] His work has been of primary importance in Brazil and has given rise to an extensive literature of the finest quality, with an analytical approach derived largely from the methods of the comparative study of cultures of social anthropology, which were very different from what was at the time called "historical method." The studies produced by those who have continued his methods are now absolutely indispensable to any further work on Negro slavery, even for those who are interested mainly in historical development and perspective. Such studies comprise, for example, Arthur Ramos' series *O problema do negro no Brasil* and the work of Gilberto Freyre and others, many of whom have been publishing in the

---

[5] On Saco and his work see Bibliography, under Saco, and Jorrín, 1944; and Corbitt, 1944.

[6] Raimundo Nina Rodriques began the publication of his analytical studies in 1896 in the *Revista Brasileira*. Essential, for example, are his *Os africanos no Brasil*, 1935a, and *O animismo fetichista dos negros bahianos*, 1935b.

4

Biblioteca de Devulgação Científica. At the present time, there is still being produced a brilliant series of studies on the Negro in Brazil from a purely sociological or from both a historical and sociological point of view by such research workers as Florestán Fernandes, Fernando Henrique Cardoso, and Octavio Ianni.[7] The same type of work has also been done by the sociologist Fernando Ortiz for Cuba and the Antilles.[8] A similar impact in the field of social anthropology and comparative culture studies has come from a group of research workers of all nationalities through work commenced a little later, with like aims and methods, on the contribution of Negro cultures in other parts of America where they are still very much a living reality. Particularly important are such books as *The Myth of the Negro Past* by Melville Herskovits, first published in 1941, and the studies of Pierre Verger, George E. Simpson, Alfred Métraux, Sidney Mintz, and Roger Bastide.[9]

As history, Saco's work did not produce any immediate result. The attention of Latin American historians was still too concentrated upon general national histories and the biographies of the heroes associated with the struggle for independence from Spain. Philosophical and ideological changes, slow and confused in many respects, from Neoclassic to Romantic norms and concepts of history and finally to a liberal and radical Positivism, made very little difference to the themes of the historians. It was only after many years, when attention became centered on a study of institutions, that the problem of Negro slavery began to undergo revision and new works on the subject began to appear. The key study in this is Georges Scelle's *La traite négrière aux Indes de Castille*, published in Paris in 1906. It is still a basic work. From the year of its publication up to the almost complete renewal of interest in the theme, which began in Latin America in the 1940s, one can discern the development of

[7] See Bibliography, under Ramos, 1943; Freyre, 1966 and 1970; Fernandes, 1971; Cardoso, 1962; and Ianni, 1962.

[8] Ortiz, 1951.

[9] Verger, 1953 and 1954; Simpson, 1941 and 1955; Métraux, 1958; Mintz, 1960a; and Bastide, 1967.

three major factors which are directly or indirectly relevant to research on the place and importance of the Negro in America.

1. From 1935 up to the present time there has been a consistent study of Spanish institutions in America. This has been useful specifically in clarifying many of the legal aspects of slavery on the one hand, and its exact place within the various institutions on the other. Particularly significant has been the work of Silvio Zavala, José María Ots Capdequí, Charles Verlinden, and José Miranda.[10]

2. A little later, the development of an ever-growing interest in economic history first, and more recently in social and demographic history obviously had to take cognizance directly or indirectly of the pertinence of slavery to such studies. The pioneering work in this respect was the important contribution to aspects of economic history made by Earl Hamilton and Clarence Haring. Following after them were the patient and laborious studies of Huguette and Pierre Chaunu, Charles Boxer, and others. Such Latin American writers as Ricardo Levene, Manuel Moreyra Paz-Soldán, Guillermo Lohmann Villena, and Eduardo Arcila Farías soon joined in studies of this kind. In social and demographic history the general studies of Angel Rosenblat and Magnus Mörner are extremely useful, as indeed are also the specialized studies of Lesley Byrd Simpson, Sherburne F. Cook, and Woodrow Borah.

3. The formation and development of national archives and the publication of the classic collections of documents of the second half of the nineteenth century had an important role in revitalizing historical research. Here and there in Latin America were published the records of the proceedings of the most important colonial town councils, followed by other, more specialized documents based on historical material from various colonial repositories. Some of those who have been responsible for this publication are Silvio Zavala, Manuel Moreyra Paz-Soldán, Richard Konetzke, Eduardo Posada, and Carlos Restrepo Canal.[11]

[10] For these writers and most of those named in the following paragraphs, see Bibliography.

[11] For Konetzke, Posada, and Canal, see Section 2 of Bibliography.

Such developments in historical methods, research, and making sources available could not have been otherwise than directly significant to the study of African slavery in Latin America, especially in the context of the growing interest in Negro cultures. A large number of studies devoted to aspects of Negro slavery in Latin America continued to be published in Europe, America, and even Africa. In Europe, after the works of Arthur Helps and Georges Scelle, there appeared various studies by Gaston Martin, León Vignols, Charles Verlinden, Antonio Domínguez Ortiz, and Frédéric Mauro. In the United States since 1916 the *Journal of Negro History* has been an extremely useful publication for those interested in Negro history and cultures. Later Frank Tannenbaum's book, *Slave and Citizen: The Negro in the Americas* came to be widely read and discussed. This and the studies of James Ferguson King, particularly, drew attention to the problem of the Negro in Latin American history. In recent years the theme has become the center of lively controversy and intense research. North American historians have taken up a number of different specializations which seem to give excellent results. Herbert Klein has concentrated on comparative studies, Eugene Genovese on an interpretation of the place of slavery in the development of capitalism, Philip Curtin on the numbers of slaves involved in the trade, and James Lockhart on the Negro groups in the colonial society of Peru. The results of other research associated either directly or indirectly with slavery have been published in different monographs or geographical studies: Richard Graham and Stanley Stein in relation to Brazil (Graham, abolition; Stein, coffee in Vassouras), Arthur Corwin for Cuba (abolition), and John Lombardi for Venezuela (slaves in the Wars of Independence and in society in the early period of the republic, and manumission). For their part each Latin American country has one or several historians who have made vital contributions through significant studies of their own areas. Such are Diego Luís Molinari, Elena Scheuss de Studer, and Carlos Sempat Assodourian in Argentina (various details of the trade and its operation); in Brazil Mauricio Goulart (a very useful history of Brazilian slavery) and Fernando Henrique Cardoso (slavery and capitalism in the south); and in Colombia Jaime Jaramillo Uribe (slaves and society in the eighteenth century and attitudes toward manumission). Others are Ramiro Guerra y Sánchez and Manuel Moreno Fraginals (the economic and social implications of sugar production) in Cuba; in Mexico, Gonzalo Aguirre Beltrán (Negro population, the slave trade, the role of Negroes in Independence); in Puerto Rico, Luis Díaz Solar (history of local slavery); Ildefonso Pereda Valdés, Eugenio Petit Muñoz, and Paulo de Carvalho-Neto in Uruguay (various aspects including culture and anthropological studies, and questions of legal, social, and economic status); and in Venezuela, Miguel Acosta Saignes (life of slaves there, the trade, and the *cimarrones*, or fugitive slaves.)

All the above writers and many others whom it has been impossible to cite have been fundamental to the writing of the brief work which follows. It is the author's hope that the summary he has undertaken will center even more interest on the problems and implications of Negro slavery in Latin America.

CHAPTER ONE

THE INTRODUCTION AND ESTABLISHMENT OF NEGRO SLAVERY

The first Negro slaves made their appearance in the New World very early, almost immediately after the discovery of America, when only a few islands of the Caribbean and odd stretches of the mainland beaches were known. They were certainly present long before the European newcomers began to form any comprehensive idea of the vast continent they had discovered.

Slavery was a well-known social and economic institution from the earliest times. It initially consisted of the enslavement of conquered peoples and captives of war. Later, individuals who had performed meritorious services were rewarded by the granting of slaves or the permission to have slaves. In the precapitalist framework of society in the European late Middle Ages, it was a simple case of the outright ownership of one human by another, to be acquired and disposed of according to circumstances. It would be more exact if we said, at the point when the great discoveries and European expansion in the world were beginning to take place, that the institution of slavery was not only well known but also time honored. It was the American experience that was to add new dimensions to it.

The effectiveness of slavery in production and economic stability had been well established in classical times, and it was to become even more obvious in the fifteenth and sixteenth centuries. In contrast, the early period of the

9

Middle Ages did not seem specifically to need slavery for its own particular type of social and economic organization. Despite this, the legal tradition that slavery had created never entirely disappeared in medieval Europe. Very early in the Christian kingdoms of the Iberian peninsula, one can find codes that stipulate the social, legal, and economic control of African slaves. In the seventh century in Visigothic Spain, the Fuero Juzgo carefully differentiated between types of work and workers.[1] Later, in the twelfth century other codes òf law and statutes—such as the Fueros of Salamanca, Soria, Cuenca, and so on—emphasized the differences between serfs, paid workers, and slaves.[2] Finally, the Siete Partidas (1256-1265) recast this ancient Castilian legal tradition within a whole legal heritage derived from the Romans, Visigoths, and Arabs.[3] The Siete Partidas were later to be taken as a fundamental legislative precedent when it came to the formulation of a body of laws designed to regulate the various aspects of Negro slavery in the New World.

[1] *Fuero*: term used to denote either a general corpus of laws (the Fuero Juzgo) or a municipal charter for financial and administrative privileges and for locally applicable laws (that of Cuenca [ca. 1189], for example). The promulgation of the laws of the Fuero Juzgo in the seventh century, as the *Liber Judiciorum* or *Liber Gothorum*, represented an attempt to reduce to one common code the differing laws and practices under which the two peoples, Visigoths and Hispano-Romans (see n. 3 below), had hitherto been living. Such laws came to form the theoretical legal basis of Castilian medieval society.

[2] See Section 2 of the Bibliography: Sánchez Ruano, 1870; Sánchez, Galo, 1919; and Ureña, 1935.

[3] The Romans had come to Spain (219-218 B.C.) as a result of their struggle with Carthage. By A.D. 409 their power was patently on the point of collapse, being by 462 completely ineffective. The Visigoths, or western half of the Gothic people, for some centuries on the move across Europe from Scandinavia, had come to Spain initially as allies of the Romans. By 456 they had firmly established themselves. The elective nature of their monarchy, howver, tended to dissensions which came to a head at the beginning of the eighth century, and this, together, with the impetus of Moslem expansion in North Africa, brought about the landing of Tarik at Gibraltar (Gebel-Tarik) in 711. By 718 the Arab victory was complete, with a small number of Visigoths and supporters in refuge behind the Cantabrian mountains in the north of Spain.

The Siete Partidas form perhaps the most encyclopedic medieval systematization of law in Europe. It is composed of seven parts or books undertaken by Alfonso the Learned, though it seems more reasonable that it was closely directed rather than written by him. See Martínez Alcubilla, 1885; Marshall, 1931; and Domínguez Ortiz, 1952.

Portuguese Explorations of the African Coast

One of the essential motives for European expansion in the fifteenth century was the production of precious metals and goods in overseas possessions for export to Europe, which had as its base compulsory work systems or slavery. Since the Azores and Canary Islands were stopping points on the route between the Iberian peninsula and the Atlantic coast of Africa, it is hardly surprising that the African slave trade should come to have a special meaning for their economy. The colonization of Madeira and the Azores had been brought about by the pressures of a highly successful commerce in slaves, sugar, gold, and spices. The greater part of the plantations and sugar mills of these islands in the fifteenth century rapidly came almost exclusively to rely on the Negro slaves imported as a result of Portuguese incursions in Africa. As a result, when Spain and Portugal came to America, there existed a new, powerful interest in the usefulness of slavery, alongside an ancient legal tradition.

On the African coast Guinea became the center of mutual rivalry. It formed the great commercial and diplomatic battleground of Iberian expansion. (See map 1). During the years of Prince Henry the Navigator, of Dom Pedro, duke of Coimbra, and especially of John II, the Portuguese gained the upper hand in the control of the African coastline.[4] In

---

[4] In 1419 the southern known limit of this coastline was the treacherous Cape Bojador (see map 1), which was only rounded after some twelve or fifteen carefully prepared expeditions. By the time Prince Henry died (1460) the Portuguese had reached Sierra Leone and had settled the Cape Verde Islands. Madeira had been explored in 1419 and settled between 1420-25. The Azores were colonized in 1445, and an expedition made to conquer the Canaries in 1424. Sugar cane was introduced to these Atlantic islands from Sicily and by 1460 it was an important crop. By 1493 Madeira had some eighty factory managers.

Dom Pedro (Henry's elder brother) was regent (1439-1446) during the minority of Alfonso V. The reign of Alfonso's successor John (João) II (1481-1495) saw the rounding of the Cape of Good Hope by Bartolomeu Dias (1488) and the overland journey of Pero de Covilhã to East Africa and India.

In 1479 by the Treaty of Alcaçovas, the Canaries were awarded to Castile in return for Castilian acceptance of Portuguese rights to the other islands and to parts of mainland Africa. Other differences in this respect were finally settled by the celebrated Treaty of Tordesillas in 1494. See Boxer, 1969b; Pérez Embid, 1949; and H. V. Livermore, *A History of Portugal* (Cambridge, 1947).

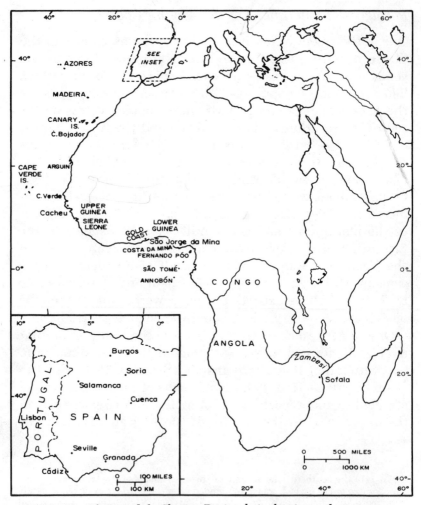

Map 1. Africa and the Iberian Peninsula in the sixteenth century.

the meantime they had been organizing from this area the initial stages of the slave trade.[5]

These years were crucial to the direction and form which colonial expansion would take. The war of Granada[6] and Columbus' discovery of the New World had the practical

---

[5] See Boxer, 1969a and 1969c; Verlinden, 1924, 1942, 1949, 1955, 1958, and 1961.

[6] 1482-1492. The fall of Granada marked the end of the reconquest of Spain from the Moors (718-1492). The reconquest had been far from a continuous sustained military effort. Its sporadic fighting and raids as well as its battles and sieges clearly encouraged slavery in the way of taking and selling captives.

effect of removing Castile from any possibility of establishing itself in either Guinea or the Congo. On the other hand, the Portuguese had gained firm control of Cape Verde by the establishment of a trading post on the island of Arguin in 1445, and the fort of São Jorge da Mina on the Gold Coast in 1482.[7] However, just as John II was ready to initiate contact with the Kingdom of the Congo for the purposes of colonization and also perhaps of conquest, other economic and colonial issues caused Portugal temporarily to lay aside its interests in African expansion. Perhaps the most telling reasons were the economic success of the sugar plantations on the island of São Tomé off the West African coast, the economic boom in the slave trade, and the first attempts to occupy the newly discovered lands of Brazil.[8] On the other hand, commercial relations between the Iberian peninsula and Moslem North Africa had been very vigorous since the fourteenth century. A continual current of commercial activity flowed through the network of posts that included Morocco, Seville, Lisbon, and Cádiz. This network was especially concerned with the trade in gold, wheat, indigo, and Moslem and Negro slaves.

One of the first and most obvious results of the discovery of the New World was the establishment of an active commerce. It was a monopolistic, closed trade, with the Iberian peninsula at its center. It was logical that this new trade should become closely integrated with Portugal's and Spain's previous commercial enterprises in Africa.[9] Seville and Lisbon were the two ports that came to play the leading role in developing the transatlantic trade route. They operated through the Canaries and the Azores as compulsory ports of call. These islands, in the sixteenth century, were still being used on the African route to Guinea. Would not this

---

[7] See map 1. The Portuguese had reached the Gold Coast in 1471. São Jorge da Mina (in present-day Ghana) was the first of a long series of coastal forts built by the Europeans in an effort to control trade, especially when the demand for slaves became intense.

[8] São Tomé, uninhabited, was discovered in 1470. Soil, climate, demand for sugar, and the extensive use of slavery accounted for its remarkable success. Production increased thirty-fold in twenty years (1530-50: from 62.5 to 1,875 short tons a year). See Boxer, 1969a; and Pérez Embid, 1948. Brazil was discovered in 1500 by the fleet of Pedro Alvares Cabral, outward bound for India.

[9] Ricard, 1955; and Mauro, 1956.

fact alone explain the presence of the first African slaves
in America? But there is more. As the sixteenth century
progressed, commerce with Morocco began to dwindle. This
meant that Cádiz, which had become more closely associated
with the Mediterranean region, was faced with the threat
of disappearing as a major trading port. It had of necessity
to enter into the commercial triangle formed by Guinea,
Lisbon, and Seville. This triangle, in its turn, came increasingly to develop the African area of its operations as it
extended itself progressively down the Atlantic coastline of
the continent.[10]

The Economics of Colonial Expansion

Despite the fact that in the immediate prediscovery period
there was a favorable economic climate for slavery as well
as legal precedents, these factors do not entirely explain the
early presence of slaves in the New World, or the subsequent
large and rapid expansion of Negro slavery. The first legislation dealing with African slaves in America was enacted nine
years after the date of its discovery. This fact is indicative
that, to all intents and purposes, both whites and blacks
arrived on American soil at the same time. The legislation
in question was promulgated in the Instrucciones by the
Spanish crown in 1501. It prohibited slaves, Jews, Moors,
and recent converts to Christianity from migrating to the
new lands. Only Christians born of Christian parents on the
peninsula were to be permitted to do so.[11] Some writers have
discussed the possibility that Negroes came to America
before the arrival of the Spaniards, either by way of a
legendary expedition undertaken by the Sultan of Guinea,

[10] H. and P. Chaunu, 1956-59, vol. VIII (1).

[11] Scelle, 1906. The converts, known as *conversos* or "New Christians," were the
result of large-scale conversions, particularly of Jews. These conversions occurred
in the century following such mob massacres as those of 1391 and the measures
taken by the crown (especially by Henry III [1390-1406] with his idea of a single
state and an exclusive spiritual authority), and in the century following the order
for the expulsion of the Jews in 1492. In 1502 the Moors of Granada, who had
been guaranteed religious freedom, were likewise given the choice between conversion
and exile.

14

Mohamed Gao, in 1300, or by other still unknown means.[12] It has been stated that Alonso Pietro, the pilot of Columbus' *La Niña*, was a mulatto. In the second half of the fifteenth century the Genoese, Portuguese, and Andalusian navigators frequently used Negro slaves in their crews. On the other hand, it seems fairly certain that some of the noblemen and gentlemen who went with Columbus on his second voyage of colonization had slaves among their retainers—hence the edict of 1501.

The importation of slaves on a large scale arose, however, from more profound economic and ideological reasons. At the beginning of the sixteenth century Fray Nicolás de Ovando imported several dozen Negroes for the mines of Hispaniola. Thereafter, starting in 1505, all the important people involved in the first Spanish possessions in the Antilles—Fernando, the son of Columbus, the friars of the Order of St. Jerome, and the licenciate Zuazo[13]—were increasingly eager to import them, even directly from Cape Verde with special licenses from the king of Portugal. Their requests emphasized the sense of importance, and even urgency, that the whole question was acquiring as the islands progressively developed the production of sugar.[14] Even Fray Bartolomé de las Casas, in those years when his opinion had more weight, supported these views. He repented, however, profoundly regretting that he had in this way encouraged the concept and practice of Negro slavery, as he himself tells us in his *History of the Indies*.[15]

[12] Mellafe, 1959.

[13] Nicolas de Ovando was appointed judge and governor of Hispaniola (1501-1509). The friars of St. Jerome, or Hieronymites (Jerónimos) were a Spanish congregation established in the fourteenth century under the Rule of St. Augustine; they were highly influential in both Spain and the New World. One of the results of Las Casas' memorial on his "community scheme" was the sending of a Hieronymite commission (1516-1520) to inquire into the whole Indian problem, to investigate government functionaries, and to implement some of the provisions of the Laws of Burgos (1512); see text below. Zuazo was appointed to the commission as its judge of inquiry. See *Colección de Documentos inéditos de ... Indias* (Madrid, 1864-84), vol. VII, pp. 14-65; and Henry R. Wagner and Helen R. Parish, *The Life and Writings of Bartolomé de las Casas* (Albuquerque, 1969), pp. 18-34.

[14] Pérez de Tudela Bueso, 1955; and Sauer, 1966.

[15] *Historia de las Indias*. For an example of his initial attitude see *Colección de Documentos inéditos de ... Indias*, vol. VII, p. 41 ("If necessary white and black slaves can be brought from Castile to keep herds, build sugar mills, wash

The petitions of these notable persons, together with those of the local municipal councils of the new towns, had in common two fundamental ideas. They stressed the need for Negro slaves in order to work the mines and wash out the gold, and they insisted that only black labor could alleviate the burden suffered by the native population in having to undertake singlehandedly the production of goods essential to European colonization. A further point was made by others, to the effect that the work output of one Negro was equivalent to that of four or even eight Indians.[16] Variations of these two ideas were basic to the whole growth of African slavery in the New World. To be associated with them is the evolution of the ideological principle of the tutelary responsibility of the Spanish crown toward the native population of its colonies. This responsibility received concrete expression for the first time in the Laws of Burgos promulgated in 1512. It developed throughout the sixteenth century and resulted eventually in strict limitations on the utilization of Indian manpower. The aim of the crown was to achieve some sort of separation between the native social substratum and its potential exploiter: the Spanish colonial society which exercised effectual control.[17]

Insofar as the Spanish colonies in America as a whole are concerned, it was in the Antilles that African slavery was first introduced and consolidated—a minute area in comparison with the eventual vast expanse of the rest of Spanish America (see map 2). In the Antilles one finds for the first time, in a more or less complete form, the social and economic

---

gold, do other things . . ."). For his review of this attitude see Book III, chap. 102 of his *Historia*; and a description of the inhumanities of the trade in Africa, Book I, chaps. 24-27. See also Wagner and Parish, pp. 22-23 (where they comment on the above passage), 38-41, and 245-47.

[16] Herrera, 1945.

[17] The first formal attack on the system of the encomiendas and forced labor (see Introduction, n. 1) was made by the Dominican Antonio de Montesinos in 1511. The result of his action was the appointment of a commission out of which came the enactment of the Laws of Burgos. Forced labor was largely retained, but the crown in a number of ways attempted to limit its abuse and explicitly reserved to itself the right to allot Indians. The development of Spanish policy vis-à-vis the native inhabitants can be studied in original sources; for example, through the publications of Lewis Hanke (see Bibliography), 1943; and Muro Orejón, 1945 and 1957. See also Hanke's *The Spanish Struggle for Justice* (Philadelphia, 1949); and J. H. Parry, *The Spanish Seaborne Empire* (London, 1966).

problems that slavery attempted to solve. As the empire expanded, the Spaniards encountered similar problems which led to the establishment of slavery throughout the New World. In fact, the Antilles were in many ways the initial center for the work of the subsequent occupation and conquest of the mainland. They formed the complementary stage to the earlier Spanish colonial experience in the Canaries, and they provided the further experience and also the resources needed to begin Spain's continental expansion. They were a testing ground. There new arrivals from Europe could become acclimatized and could introduce new animals and plants. Methods of political control, of production, and of policies and administration for the Indian population were tried out in the islands.[18] For Negro slavery, however, the most important feature of the Caribbean experience was the problem of the native inhabitants and their inability to provide manpower.

The Indian population of the islands was of relatively low density when it received the first impact of European expansion, at least when one compares it with the population density of the Andes and Mexico.[19] Furthermore, it lacked completely the notion of producing over and above immediate needs; production was limited to only what was required for subsistence and for ceremonial purposes. Clearly under these circumstances, the Indians of the Antilles were far less able than the great native civilizations of the mainland to bear the brunt of compulsory systems of work in the first years of European occupation. The Indians were faced not only with an increase in the number of hours and in the total energy spent on working but with a change in diet together with a decrease in the amount of food consumed, and with hitherto unknown diseases.[20]

There were other historical circumstances which contributed to a worsening of a situation already on the point of a complete demographic and social collapse. The Antilles, besides being a center for Spanish acclimatization and for

[18] Sauer, 1966.
[19] Cook and Borah, 1960a, 1960b, 1971; and Rosenblat, 1954.
[20] Cook and Borah, 1971; and Mellafe, 1965a.

17

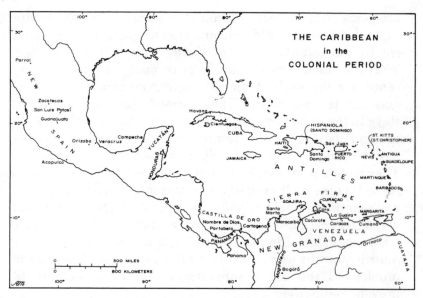

Map 2. The Caribbean in the colonial period.

the gaining of colonial experience, also constituted the initial base for conquest on an extensive, continental scale. The islands therefore had to provide both the supplies needed for such an undertaking and part of the indispensable capital or accumulated goods required to finance it. The implications were particularly serious in that, unlike Mexico, Colombia, or Peru, the Indians had not accumulated precious metals, either for ceremonial uses or for motives of social distinction. Gold, one of the motivating forces of European expansion, could only be obtained by placer working of the gold-bearing sands in the islands. The fundamental feature of this period, then, is the quest for gold. Gold formed the basis of the first economic stage of colonial rule in America, certainly an ill-fated stage for the native population of the Caribbean, and one to be subsequently repeated throughout the continent.[21]

In addition to laboring intensively for gold, the Indians were expected to provide both domestic service for Spanish colonial society and auxiliary personnel for the work of discovery and conquest. More manpower was required to

[21] H. and P. Chaunu, 1956-1959, vol. VIII, (1); Meza, 1941; and Mellafe, 1959.

produce food, care for livestock, transport goods, and so on. Later on, even more workers were needed to develop the silver mines or to man the sugar mills and plantations. A large estate (*ingenio*) required at the very least eighty workers to cultivate and process sugar cane; a smaller estate (*trapiche*) between thirty and forty.[22] The native population, singlehanded, simply could not stand up to the immense burden of all these demands. The case of the island of Hispaniola is eloquent. When the Spaniards arrived it must have had a native population of approximately a million. In 1508 it had only 60,000; in 1554, 30,000; and so on, until in 1570 contemporary documents show a population of scarcely 500.[23] In general, this rapid and drastic reduction of the Indian population, with variations in actual figures, causes, and the years involved, became characteristic of the rest of Spanish America. In an effort to solve the fundamental scarcity of manpower in the Antilles, various solutions, which coexisted side by side for many years, were tried out. One was the immigration of colonists from Spain. Another was the importation of the natives from regions which had not yet been occupied, and who in fact, were little more than slaves or semi-slaves. But the two solutions which prevailed, and which were the most important throughout the second half of the sixteenth century, if not before, were the paid employment of mestizos, and the massive importation of African slaves.[24] Thus, at the beginning of Spanish expansion in America, the institution of African slavery was introduced to the Antilles as the imperative solution to a shortage of labor created by the inherent necessities of the expansion itself.

In the Portuguese possessions in Brazil, forces similar to those operating in the Spanish colonies of the Antilles

[22] Las Casas, 1951.

[23] The author (see Mellafe, 1959), on the basis of documents from the first half of the sixteenth century, calculated that the initial native population must have been at least 100,000. However, later studies have tended to augment this figure greatly (as in fact they have done for other native populations living in similar conditions and utilizing like technologies). Sherburne Cook and Woodrow Borah (1971) discuss the population of Hispaniola in their chap. 6; here they even suggest a figure of 8 million as being possible on the arrival of the Europeans.

[24] Zavala, 1948. The term *mestizo* in this book follows newer Latin American usage in covering any racial mixture, rather than earlier usage in which it referred specifically to an Indian-white mixture.

created a like demand for slaves. But there were also some major differences, which are all the more significant if one bears in mind that Portugal controlled, if not the entire slave trade, at least the most important ports and the greater part of those regions in Africa where slaves were obtained. Because of the latter one could perhaps quite reasonably assume that, in supplying African slaves, its possessions in Brazil would have had first priority. But this was not in fact true, at least until fairly late in the colonial period.

The landholders or *donatarios* who obtained grants in Brazil from the Portuguese crown wanted to repeat there the success which their compatriots had already had in producing sugar on the African coast and in the islands off Africa.[25] Instead, they found insuperable problems. The first of these arose as a result of the indifference of the crown and of the merchants of the kingdom. Portugal, in achieving its remarkable commercial and colonial expansion with relatively limited home resources, had become exhausted. In Africa and India its expansion was based on trading posts and forts rather than on an active colonization. To maintain this system was much more important to Portugal than was the uncertain colonization of the New World. One reason was that Brazil had so far not appeared to possess either precious metals or other elements of real value to international commerce at that time. There were none of the dazzling finds in the way of advanced cultures and great sources of wealth which had characterized the Spanish continental conquests. Although a limited number of sugar plantations on the northeast coast of Brazil had had very good results, their success had been at once followed by great difficulties:

[25] John (João) III of Portugal divided Brazil into fifteen captaincies which he distributed among twelve donatarios. This system created a hierarchy of landlords with certain rights (taxes, law, justice, appointments, and land distribution), and likewise certain obligations. They were expected to defend their captaincies from attack and, theoretically, foster imperial trade; only the king had the ultimate right of limiting and regulating their powers. See E. Bradford Burns, *A History of Brazil* (New York and London, 1970). Other useful works are Prado, 1971, and for official and unofficial documents of Brazilian history (1494-1964), Bradford Burns' edition of *A Documentary History of Brazil* (New York, 1966). Burns believes that the first known full cargo of slaves to be directly shipped from Africa was unloaded in Brazil by Jorge Lopes Bixorda, in 1538. This shipload is apart from the earlier slaves brought to Brazil from Portugal—a point to be taken up later in the text.

lack of capital, shortage of labor, and problems arising out of the international market in sugar.

In the first half of the sixteenth century, the marketing and distribution of sugar, and also the best techniques for its refining, were controlled by Italian merchants, especially the Genoese and Venetians. During the second half of the century Dutch merchants operating from Antwerp and Amsterdam began to enter the market.[26] At this precise moment the supply of Negroes to Brazil started to increase, because of the action of Dutch capital and Dutch merchants.

The first Africans in Brazil came, mostly by way of Lisbon, with the landholders who traveled to take up their grants in the new territory. These Negroes, like their counterparts in the colonies established by the Spanish conquerors on the American mainland, formed a special group and were considered as servants and as allies of the occupation rather than simply as manpower.

On the other hand, the use of the Indians for the sugar mills and the plantations involved exactly the same problem as in the Antilles: a drastic decrease of population. But the case of Brazil was further complicated because the Indians there adopted a much more rebellious and aggressive attitude than had the natives of Hispaniola. There were also massive flights of Indians into the interior of the continent.[27]

For decades planters, business promoters, cities, and even the Church brought as much pressure as they could upon the homeland for slaves. But their petitions and requests elicited no response. The Portuguese crown and the traders in African slaves were more interested in providing the Spanish possessions with Negroes since they were paid in silver and gold. Also, on the east coast of Africa, there was apparently developing an export trade in ivory and gold rather than slaves. This was carried out at first through Sofala, and later by way of the Zambesi River.[28]

Things began to change once the control of the sugar market ceased to be the exclusive preserve of Italian merchants. In 1550 the city of Salvador da Bahia received a

[26] Deer, 1949-50.
[27] See, for example, Fernandes, 1970.
[28] Goulart, 1949; and Boxer, 1969a and 1969c.

shipment of Negroes directly from Africa for distribution among its inhabitants. In 1559, the Regent, Dona Catarina, ordered her representative in São Tomé to hand over slaves to every sugar producer who had the appropriate papers issued by the governor of Brazil.[29] This order could be considered the first official act on the part of the Portuguese crown to protect the sugar interests of its colony. From the 1560s commercial agreements between planters and Portuguese and Dutch merchants to import small shipments of slaves became common. This trade, however, was still only relatively minor. Specialists in this field estimate that in the whole of the sixteenth century no more than 40 or 50 thousand black slaves were imported into Brazil. The Spanish colonies imported an equivalent number in less than one decade.[30]

Privileges, Exemptions, and Annuities Granted by the Spanish Crown

The fundamental factors involved in the consolidation of Negro slavery in America were clearly Spanish legal precedents, demographic problems, the shortage of manpower, and the capabilities of Sevillian and Portuguese commerce in developing extensive trade routes along the coasts of Africa. However, one must add a number of other considerations. At least insofar as Spain is concerned, an enormous importance was attached to private initiative and capital in the actual work of the conquest up to about 1570. As a result the monarch and the Council of the Indies found themselves obliged to grant certain privileges, guarantees, and exemptions to those who undertook this work, as a recompense for their efforts and investment. This obligation often directly involved Negro slavery. Hernado Cortes and Francisco Pizarro, for example, besides being given leave to conquer Mexico and Peru, were also granted permission to import considerable numbers of black slaves into both areas. Preci-

[29] Goulart, 1949. Dona Catarina, the Queen, had been appointed regent on the death of her husband, John (João) III in 1557. The successor to the throne, the ill-fated Sebastian, was then just three.

[30] A good source for such estimates is Curtin, 1969.

22

sely the same thing applied, though to a lesser degree, to the conquerors of the other regions of Spanish America.[31]

Almost all the officials appointed by the Council of the Indies in the sixteenth century were granted permits to take a number of slaves, usually between three and eight, with them to the New World. The officials included viceroys, governors, judges of the high court, founders of new towns and settlements, ecclesiastical dignitaries, and even parish priests. The motive behind this ruling was that most of these officials were prohibited from using the services of the native inhabitants for domestic or commercial purposes. They were not required to pay any fee for their license to import these slaves, and though officially they were not permitted to sell them, in practice this prohibition was never strictly enforced. This mechanism for the importation of African slaves proved to be one of the surest and cheapest ways of maintaining a small market in them, even in the most unexpected places in the New World.

The Negro slave as an object of trade came with the conquest itself, not after it. Slaves were sold and bought in all the Spanish armies wherever they were to be found—in the siege of Tenochtitlán (Mexico City), at the capture of the Inca Atahualpa in Peru, or crossing the Andes on the way to Chile. Accompanying the activity of conquest there was always the commercial activity of trading in slaves. The men who equipped the various expeditions, generally the captains themselves, would include slaves in their baggage trains. These slaves, who had been obtained by royal privilege, would then be sold at high prices if the expedition turned out to be profitable to those taking part in it.[32]

The granting of prerogatives in fact went much further. The policy of the crown involved not only conquest of new lands but also their subsequent social and economic restructuring. To accomplish this entailed the granting of still more privileges and guarantees. Such a guarantee, insofar as the

[31] Aguirre Beltrán, 1946; Mellafe, 1959; and Friede, 1960.

[32] Mellafe, 1954 and 1959. There are a large number of documentary examples of the above. See Bibliography under U.S. Library of Congress, *The Harkness Collection*, 1932 and 1936, for Peru; and Millares Carlo and Mantecón, 1945-1946, for Mexico.

institution of slavery was concerned, was the stipulation that in certain circumstances slaves could not be seized for non-payment of debts, for example, if they were indispensable to the operation of a sugar mill or a mine, or if the debt was in favor of the king. Conquistadors could have all their goods confiscated for debts, with the exception of their bed, a horse, and two slaves. In Peru and Chile, a mine could be kept by whoever at the time held it by virtue of usufruct or concession if it was what was known as *poblada* or occupied by people, that is to say, in this particular context, worked by eight Indians or by four Negroes.[33]

Besides the general economic policy of the crown, there were also one or two particular features which even more directly fostered the development of slavery as a typical institution of the conquest. One of the most important was the granting of annuities or pensions. In the early decades of the sixteenth century, the Spanish crown, always in economic difficulties, would confiscate the remittances of specie which had been sent to Spain in the annual fleets from the Indies. These sums were privately owned by individuals, usually conquistadors or merchants. To compensate for such forced loans, the crown would pay a relatively high rate of interest in the form of annuities. They were thus rather like the payment of an I.O.U. or promissory note drawn against the public debt. The particular point about these annuities is that for a period of many years they were frequently converted into permits to import Negro slaves into the colonies. It became a thoroughly profitable business which attracted many of those who had become wealthy from the conquest.[34]

The system of annuities directly linked the great conquistadors, who were in fact also the entrepreneurs of the conquest, with the institution of African slavery. The first conquerors in every region of America were both the first importers of slaves and the most important owners of Negro

---

[33] Encinas, 1945, vol. II; and Levene, 1927-1929, vol. I.

[34] It was not only possible to convert such annuities into licenses, but their payment also came to involve other sources of revenue collected by the crown. A good explanation of these points can be found in Ulloa, 1963. For relevant examples see also Haring, 1939; and Mellafe, 1959.

manpower. In the eight years between 1529 and 1537, the two brothers, Francisco and Hernando Pizarro, who were considered by the Spanish crown to be the men most responsible for the conquest of Peru, were granted licenses to import 262 slaves into the area. At the same time, another twenty-two conquistadors also received permits, though for far fewer slaves. It is worth pointing out how contemporaneous was the importation of slaves with the actual conquest and occupation of Peru. In 1529 territorial occupation as such had not yet begun, and in 1537 it had not yet finished. The city of Lima, the main center of the Spanish colonial establishment in Peru, was founded in 1535. It is also interesting to note that the two Pizarro brothers, by annuities and other concessions, actually obtained licenses to import more than the 262 slaves mentioned above, and that these licenses were doubtless sold to the merchants of various nations who were at the time stationed in Seville.[35]

Racial Alliances and the Attitudes of the Conquistadors

The entire colonial situation in America seemed to form a favorable set of circumstances for Negro slavery quickly to become rooted in the social and economic pattern: tradition, the possibilities offered by various trading routes, the lack of labor in some parts of the New World, and the economic policy of the homeland. One should also approach the problem of slavery from yet another point of view: the person of the conquistador himself. He was obviously audacious, partly the product of the Renaissance in his views, a capitalist and business entrepreneur. His attitude toward slaves, apart from their being objects of trade, are undeniably pertinent. African slavery was not only an economic phenomenon. One can clearly distinguish between the black slave as manpower and the black slave as companion and assistant of the conquistador. While the first centers of European colonization in the Caribbean were exerting pressure to obtain slaves so as to secure a more steady production, other groups of Negroes were participating in the various

[35] Mellafe, 1959.

expeditions of discovery and conquest. They, as well as the Spaniards, experienced the Indian resistance to their advance. It could be said that they also felt themselves to be invaders and conquerors, and in fact they were. They felt this to the point of believing themselves to have the special right also to enjoy the results of conquest and to act as victors. What is more, the conquistadors did not deny them this right. The institution of slavery, in the same general area and at the same time, was thus developing in two different ways.

The Indians on the mainland, who had resisted the Spaniards or who were suffering the consequences of subsequent Spanish rule, could easily distinguish between the Europeans and Africans. However, on the level of ordinary everyday life, there were to all intents and purposes no major differences. The Negroes were certainly in a subordinate position, but were nonetheless allied with the whites. Both groups together, white and black, utilized the conquered native peoples in the same tyrannical way. Those slaves who participated in the conquest were quite willing to become allies of the Spaniards and their active helpers. Many of them gained their liberty as a result. Others even acquired the same status as the conquistadors themselves, and could in their turn possess slaves.

This possibility explains many of the special features of Negro slavery at the time. The initial contacts between Indians and Negroes were always violent. This was true to the point that the first legislation relating to slavery which was promulgated in America tried to protect the native population against the abuses and cruelties of the Negroes.[36] The social acceptability of these slaves included marriage between conquistadors, or their sons, and Negro or mulatto slave women. In a lesser number of cases it included marriage between Negroes and the mestizo daughters of the conquistadors. In this way, and as a result of commercial dealings, grants of Indians, and so on, these groups became wealthy, coming to form an essential part of colonial upper-class society. They are obviously to be clearly differentiated from

[36] Mellafe, 1959, and Gibson, 1964. See also chap. 5 of the present work.

the African slaves who afterwards arrived in great number as laborers.[37]

The case just outlined cannot be extended to all periods or to all places on the American continent. It applies to an ethnic alliance between Negro slaves and Europeans at the time when the Europeans were conquering and consolidating their power over the native peoples. By the 1570s, in such places as Bolivia, Peru, Chile, and Mexico, where the process had once been very important, it was no longer possible for a slave to obtain his liberty and subsequently achieve an eminent place in society. In fact, in the societies which were of this type, the upper levels of the social pyramid were becoming more and more mixed with mestizo or Indian blood. This had a whitening effect. Black persons of good social status were rapidly becoming white mestizos. They did not establish separate family groups or separate communities in the regions where they lived. The white society of the conquistadors accepted them once and for all, and soon considered them also to be white.

A similar situation also occurred in Brazil during the first decades of the century, but in a much more modest way. Here, at that time, the more telling factor was the attraction of black and mulatto women as concubines for the Portuguese, rather than the acceptance of male Negroes as temporary allies in conquest and territorial expansion. However, if racial alliance and the social acceptability of Negroes in Brazil in the early part of the sixteenth century has to be qualified to some extent, it simply did not occur at all in the Spanish islands of the Caribbean and in the English, Dutch, and French colonies. Perhaps it is no mere coincidence that it is precisely in these regions that one finds a history of strong racial segregation. Other pertinent factors can be added. In the zones just mentioned, there was no long and bloody confrontation between the Europeans and the native peoples. These regions did not have a high Indian population density, or, if it was high, it quickly disappeared. Such regions were centers of plantations and tropical culti-

[37] There are numerous examples of free Negroes attaining high social standing in the sixteenth century. For some of these see Mendiburu, 1874-1890; Thayer Ojeda, 1939-1941; Mellafe, 1959; and Gibson, 1964.

vation which reached the peak of their development later, after the sixteenth century.

The conquistador himself, as a person, was very much molded by the circumstances of the Spanish conquest of the mainland. Particularly relevant were the private effort and private economic interest that it involved, the exercise of power in a situation of relative autonomy, and the recognition granted by the crown to those who had so actively promoted the conquest and who had added so much to its domains. The conquistador was turbulent, authoritarian, and energetic. He was above all a combination of conqueror, *encomendero*, and businessman.[38] He was quite prepared to accept, patronize, and enjoy the fruits of the institution of slavery. The attitude of the crown, both in granting compensation for services rendered and in economic matters, further fostered his tendency toward the use of Negro slavery. A conquistador frequently bought Negro slaves, even when he manifestly did not need them. There were two things which every important conquistador considered essential to his baggage train, army, or small retinue: his horse and his African slaves.

This trait is amply clear from the documentary evidence of the time. Particular sources are the certified bills of sale and the testimonials of merit and of services rendered. The bills of sale reflect the economic life of the very early days of the Spanish colonies, the commercial transactions of the soldiers at the very moment of the conquest itself or immediately after it. By far the most common transaction recorded on these bills is the sale of a horse or a Negro slave.[39] The second type of document is the testimonials. In themselves, they are classic items in the field of Hispanic-American historiography. They were formulated by the conquistadors whenever they sought a favor from the king or from some other important official body, or whenever any judical process made it necessary to verify their ancestry, economic and social good standing, and their conduct. These docu-

[38] *Encomendero*, the holder of an encomienda (see Introduction, n. 1, and chap. 1, n. 17).

[39] Lohmann Villena, 1941-1944; and Millares Carlo and Mantecón, 1945-1946.

ments always included, as a major, obligatory item, the details of the services rendered to the king during the conquest, the personal expenses borne, and the material damages suffered. Under the item of expenses, the purchase of horses and of Negro slaves was continually mentioned, and under damages the death of some horse or of some Negro slave.[40]

Geographical Distribution of Slaves in Latin America

A clear distinction should be drawn between the general geographical area throughout which Negro slavery initially spread and those particular regions where it came to predominate. Many writers who are not particularly specialized in this field, give an oversimplified explanation for the fact that certain Latin American countries at present completely lack any notewrothy population of Negroes, either pure blooded or mixed. They say simply that the climate of such-and-such a country or region was unsuitable for those of African extraction, or that a particular zone was so poor in the colonial period that the Europeans who occupied it were unable to bring the slave trade into their area.

However, it should be clear from our analysis that Negro slavery spread rapidly to all the regions and corners of the mainland at the same rate as the conquest itself, and that it occupied in this way the same general geographical area as did the Europeans. The habit of using black slaves to complement the crews of ships meant that they also participated in distant voyages of discovery. For example, slaves sailed across the Pacific and to regions which were only explored rather than at once occupied, as the Strait of Magellan.[41] Up to the mid-sixteenth century, the Negroes spread, as allies and auxiliaries in the conquest, to all those parts of the continent which were visited and occupied by the Europeans. In the final decades of the century, one begins to notice a more or less characteristic distribution of the

[40] A good example of such credentials has been published by Medina, 1889-95 and 1914. See also *Revista del Archivo Nacional del Perú*, vol. I, 1920. Ancestry (*limpieza de sangre*, purity of blood) was a major preoccupation not only from a social, class, or racial standpoint but also from that of proving stock as being Old Christian.

[41] Mellafe, 1959.

black population and of its subsequent mixing with mestizos. In the seventeenth century this distribution became clearly defined, and finally became fixed in the last century of the colonial period. The late colonial pattern has changed little up to the present.

The primary role in this process was certainly not climate alone. It was rather, as will become obvious in later chapters, a question of the economic base of each region, the availability of local, native labor, and the economic policies imposed by the homeland. However, there were in fact circumstances in which climate was important to slavery. The reasons are not whether it would adversely or otherwise affect people of African extraction, for they can live in quite normal physiological conditions in any latitude. There were, however, three economic and social situations, fundamental to the history of Latin America, in which climate was involved. The first of these was the interrelation of climate, production, and manpower. The second was associated with the first, but with factors added by the slaves themselves as they reacted against the oppression of slavery. This entailed an aggressive and warlike marginal existence for groups of Negro slaves. Sometimes this marginalization became absolute in the sense that the fugitives no longer had any contact at all with the normal population centers. The third situation, besides all these factors, involved the continual harassment and state of siege to which the other European powers subjected the Spanish Empire, while at the same time plantation economies were developing in the non-Spanish regions of the Caribbean. Included, then, is the occupation of part of the Antilles by England, France, and Holland. We shall examine briefly the various circumstances set out above.

If we want to understand in a proper historical sequence how the black population became distributed over the various parts of Latin America, we must start with the question of climate, production, and labor. The major population concentrations of the pre-Columbian era were in the more temperate zones, for example, in the highlands of the Andes or on the central Mexican plateau. The tropical lowlands along the coasts or in the interior, especially in

30

South America, had a much lower population density, and were more open to such factors as the spread of hitherto unknown diseases among the native population. The inhabitants of these areas were the first to disappear on contact with the Europeans. Their near extinction had an important consequence in the Spaniards' loss of a convenient source of manpower. This loss, together with the high productive potential of the lowlands and the interest in tropical one-crop economies, inevitably resulted in an extensive forced transfer of native populations in the sixteenth century. But this practice eventually had to be suspended because of the high death rate it entailed. Also involved were the legislation enacted to protect the native peoples and the opposition of settlers in the higher elevations who were thus deprived of their source of manpower. There were places where the decline of the original population was so drastic that it proved difficult, if not impossible, to compensate for it by internal relocation of Indians. Such regions were Brazil, the coasts, of Venezuela and Colombia, parts of Central America, and southern Mexico. The obvious alternative to these difficulties was the massive utilization of Negro slaves. Such a course was largely feasible because of the higher economic output of African slave labor and the profitable nature of tropical agricultural products. This is the explanation for the present high proportion of Negro and semi-Negro populations to be found in the tropical lowlands of the continent.

Keeping in mind the highlands provides the explanation why the great, historic mining centers of the mainland were seldom worked by Negro slaves. Such mines as Potosí and Huancavelica in Peru, and Zipaquirá in Colombia, were surrounded by native populations of high density, which were more protected than were the lowland ones from such demographic disasters as those that took place in the Antilles. (See map 3.) The Andean mines, then, were worked by Indians; they could not have been productive in any other way.[42]

The second situation involving climate and the distribution of the black population in Latin America is associated

[42] These are themes which will be taken up again in chap. 4.

31

Map 3. South America in the colonial period.

with the escape or violent resistance of many Negroes, once they had been landed in America, as a reaction to enslavement. Alonso González de Nájera, an intelligent observer of the Chilean scene at the beginning of the seventeenth century and of the war against the Araucanian Indians, strongly argued for the greater work capacity of the Negro as against that of the Indian. He praises the physical and mental qualities of the blacks but then adds that they had a propensity toward escaping, or even of taking up arms against the whites. He goes on to say that in Chile this tendency could not pose a severe problem since, in contrast to the tropical regions, the slaves would have no choice but to take refuge among the mountain snows, which were a difficult place to subsist in, especially if one were on the run.[43] González de Nájera was wrong insofar as there were in fact occasional bands of escaped slaves at lower altitudes in Chile, who attacked travelers and haciendas, but he is right in that there were never large numbers of them and that they never constituted a permanent danger in the colony. What he has to say in regard to Chile, however, is in stark contrast to the innumerable statements made by the authorities, chroniclers, and travelers in describing different tropical regions at different times. Frequently alarmed, they depict the danger posed by escaped slaves, who formed free villages and who lived by constant pillage of the settled areas.[44]

In Spanish runaway slaves were called by a special word, *cimarrones*, and their small villages or communities were called *palenques*, *quilombos*, or even republics. Since they formed no part of either the society or the economy of the time, they were marginal groups. Some lived in a state of war and were constantly attacking the adjacent settled areas, while others withdrew altogether to subsist in almost inaccessible, remote regions never occupied by the Europeans. The latter were truly marginal both in the geographical and

[43] See Bibliography, Section 2: González de Nájera, 1970. González de Nájera served in Chile from 1601 to 1607. The Araucanian tribes were famous for their resistance to conquest; before the arrival of the conquistadors, their fierceness had prevented the Incas from moving south of the River Maule (see map 3). They were partly assimilated during the colonial period (the Picunche and Huilliche), but the Mapuche, pushed back to the lands beyond the Bío Bío River, were not finally conquered until the 1860s. Santiago itself was saved during one of their rebellions (1553) only by the death of their leader and an epidemic of smallpox. Many Araucanians crossed over to Argentina, to form a thriving native society there.

[44] See, for example, Gage, 1969; and Lavaysse, 1967.

33

in the social sense. The cimarrones increased in number for a time in the eighteenth century. Living in any of these marginal ways, such slaves notably widened the base of Negro population distribution in the New World. Groups of them settled in the most unexpected places, always tropical, from the coasts of Peru and Ecuador to the northernmost limits of Mexico. However, they tended to concentrate in the northern and coastal provinces of Colombia and Venezuela, along the coasts of Central America, in the coastal belts and remote interior regions of the Portuguese possessions in Brazil, and particularly in some of the islands of the Caribbean.

These communities or quilombos were formed in various ways: from slave ship wrecks, from individual or mass escapes of slaves, or from short-lived European occupation of islands or coastal regions. These settlements of ex-slaves frequently existed for more than a century without any significant contact with the colonial authorities or the official commercial life of the colonies. In many places the Negroes became mixed with Indian tribes who represented the last vestiges of native cultures in these regions. (Examples would be the Chocó in Colombia, the Goajira Peninsula, the islands of Cuba and Santo Domingo during the sixteenth century, and the middle ranges of the Brazilian river system.) The resulting racial mixtures were given special names, as, for example, on some small islands of the Caribbean, where the people were called black Caribs.[45] Such contacts resulted in some significant cultural transferences between the two races some years before the major rush that was to develop in the slave trade. The slaves brought plants, seeds, small animals, and some of their utensils with them from Africa. For example, the first Negroes who came from Guinea introduced a species of the yam and certain types of African poultry. On the other hand, the Indian people in Haiti taught the Africans how to make cassava bread and various fermented beverages. Because of the lack of iron in Latin America at the beginning of the sixteenth century, the Africans had to adopt the Indian

[45] Lavaysse, 1967. Part of Goajira (see map 3) once belonged to Venezuela. Today it is entirely Colombian.

34

methods of breaking the soil with sharp-pointed wooden implements.[46]

The occupation of a number of the Caribbean islands by other European powers had political and economic consequences which must be added to what has already been said in regard to the distribution of the Negro population in America. Groups of runaway slaves had already occupied a good part of the Antilles by the time the English, French, and Dutch came to the islands. However, many of the fugitive groups were eventually absorbed, killed, or expelled by the European newcomers.

The Spaniards in the sixteenth century called Panama the throat of the Viceroyalty of Peru. This in a sense was true, not only as regards Peru, but also most of the Spanish possessions in South America and a good part of Central America. The analogy could perhaps be extended by describing the Caribbean as the mouth of the region through which one reached almost all the Spanish colonies in continental America. This zone thus became the favorite target for the incursions of Spain's enemies in the sixteenth and part of the seventeenth centuries. Pirates and buccaneers were especially attracted to the Spanish fleets from the Indies and to a number of the prosperous coastal towns. Initially, there were no serious, sustained efforts on the part of other European powers to establish themselves in any of the Caribbean islands. Besides, Spain itself at the time was well able to prevent any such attempts.

However, in the seventeenth century the situation began to change significantly, and the occupation of many of the Caribbean islands became inevitable, for a number of important reasons. The first was the growing inability of Spain to maintain complete control within the geographical bounds of its colonial empire. This became obvious, not only from the scarcity of strategic and economic resources, but also from the resulting diplomatic maneuvers. As early as 1596, France, England, and the Netherlands formed an alliance against Spain when they signed the Treaty of The Hague.

[46] Sauer, 1966.

This was the first step leading to Spain's suffering a crucial defeat and having to sign separate treaties with each country. These treaties gave Spain's enemies the opportunity to avail themselves of the legal principle that only actual occupation of territory gave lawful title to control. As a result, the Spaniards began the construction of coastal fortifications at Havana, Cartagena, and Portobelo, indicating their intention to hold the lands they already occupied rather than to try to keep the islands they had not yet settled.

The second reason leading to the establishment of other European powers in the area was commercial. The wealthy Spanish and Portuguese colonies, with a constantly growing white and mestizo population, were from the beginning of the seventeenth century a good market for manufactured goods of all types. Nationals of other European countries could only carry on this trade illicitly, but local Spanish officials often permitted it or even participated in it. Payment for foreign goods was made in gold and silver, and also in such products as sugar, cacao, tobacco, and dyes. When Dutch and English companies began to get more access to the slave trade, it too came to constitute one of the elements in foreign commerce with the Caribbean. All those involved in this commerce—merchants, crews, and slaves—needed some place to land and take on supplies. Also, it was necessary to store many of the products which had been received as payment so as to later dispatch them in bulk across the Atlantic. The almost unpopulated islands of the Caribbean made ideal harbors and warehouses.

The final reason involves the transformation of the storage centers in the islands into areas of active production in the mid-seventeenth century, as the result of an increasing demand for tropical products in Europe, not only for sugar but later for tobacco and cotton. However, sugar can again be taken as an appropriate example. Through their temporary occupation of Northeastern Brazil, the Dutch acquired a virtual monopoly of world sugar production and also learned the techniques of cultivating and refining sugar cane. They then transferred their specialized knowledge and experience to the Antilles, where they imparted the benefit of both to the other European nations in the area, especially after 1654, when they were finally expelled from Brazil. Thus the Caribbean, which had been used for the storage of goods involved in foreign commerce, including African slaves, also became an area where tropical products were cultivated.

With such incentives the settlement of the Caribbean islands was rapid. In 1626 the English and French both established themselves on the island of St. Kitts. After a number of unsuccessful attempts and some vacillations, the English spread through Barbados, Nevis, Antigua, and Jamaica. The French settled in Santo Domingo (Haiti), Guadeloupe, and Martinique. In the last decades of the century, the English possessions alone had more than 200 mills with a minimum annual production of 22,046 short tons of refined sugar, which needed 1,300 ships a year to move it. At the end of the century, the crowns of England and France regarded sugar as their most important colonial product. The Dutch made their first attempts to settle in the region in 1627, but it was not until 1634 that they established themselves firmly in Curaçao.[47]

The few settlements of freed slaves and cimarrones who had taken refuge on these islands were driven off to other islands, or were exterminated or absorbed by the new plantations. The economic and political situation depicted here was the final factor in determining the spread of the Negro population in the New World.[48]

[47] There is an extensive bibliography on the establishment of other powers in the Caribbean and their effect on Negro slavery and the development of a plantation economy. See Haring, 1910; Esquemeling, 1923; Newton, 1933; Crouse, 1940; von Lippmann, 1941-42; and Williams, 1970.

[48] Other interesting approaches, usually by geographers, to the question of Negro population distribution in Latin America can be found, for example, in Zelinsky, 1949; Moreno Toscano, 1968; and Sternberg, 1970.

CHAPTER TWO

DEVELOPMENT AND FORMS
OF THE SLAVE TRADE

The Period of Slave Licenses

Numerous extant documents make it quite obvious that the initial aim of the Spanish crown was to retain most of the African slaves imported into America for royal use. Relatively few of them were intended for the colonists in the towns or in rural areas. However, pressures exerted by the citizens and public officials of the New World to obtain a greater supply of slaves brought about a fundamental change of policy. This was marked in 1513 by the establishment of a fee of two ducats for each slave taken to the Indies, which in practice meant that African slaves could be imported into the colonies, but only with a prior license. Such licenses formed the first step in the introduction of the slave trade on a grand scale. They were also the beginning of an unexpected source of revenue for the crown, and one which was to become more and more utilized. This system, from that moment on, was an economic and political instrument of great importance. By 1578, the price of each license had risen to 30 ducats.[1]

Soon the demand for licenses increased so much that the Portuguese traders who brought African slaves to Seville were unable to meet the demand. It became convenient to get slaves from Africa in a more speedy and expeditious way. The main difficulty was that the areas forming the sources

[1] Mellafe, 1959.

38

of supply were held by Portuguese companies and merchants. So recourse was had to European bankers and merchants who had commercial dealings with the Portuguese. A crisis occurred in 1518, when Charles V gave the first exclusive trading license to one of his favorites, Laurent de Gouvenot. This license expired in 1528, and in the following year Charles granted a similar one to two representatives of the firm of the Welsers, Heinrich Ehinger and Hieronymus Seiler. These two also gained a mining concession in the province of Santa Marta on the northern Colombian coast.[2] The granting of such licenses established some important precedents. In the first place, they authorized the importation of a large number of slaves in a precise period of time. The first license was for 4,000 African slaves in five years. The second was for the same number in four years. A further precedent was that the crown reserved the right to specify both the region from which the slaves were to be obtained,and the region in America to which they were to be taken for sale. The first two licenses specified that they were to be procured from Guinea, or any other convenient place in Africa, and sold in the islands of Cuba, Hispaniola, and Jamaica, or on the mainland of Yucatán or Mexico. Mexico was in the final years replaced by what was known as Castilla del Oro (the southern part of the Central American isthmus).

Although import licenses, annual import quotas, and distribution according to zones or administrative areas were new developments for the Spanish colonies, they had already

[2] Aguirre Beltrán, 1946; and Friede, 1955-57 (see Section 2 of Bibliography). On the slaves imported into Mexico, their prices, and their quality, see Brady, 1968. For Santa Marta, see map 2.

Charles V (1500-1558), elected Holy Roman Emperor in 1519, brought the Hapsburg dynasty to Sapin (as Charles I, 1516-1556). He was the grandson of Ferdinand and Isabel, the "Catholic Monarchs". His European interests were extensive (Netherlands, Austria, Italy, and rights over Hungary and Bohemia); but on the other hand his reign marked the period of major Spanish conquest (Mexico, Guatemala, El Salvador, Peru), exploration (Magellan, La Plata, Florida, the coasts of the Gulf of Mexico and California), and colonization (the founding of Lima, 1535; Buenos Aires, 1536; and Santiago, 1541).

Also important was the exploitation of new economic resources (e.g., discovery of silver at Guanajuato and Zacatecas, 1548; and at Potosí, 1545), besides the development of the administrative machinery and institutions entailed by such expansion. The Welsers were an Augsburg banking firm with whom Charles had incurred heavy debts for his election as Holy Roman Emperor, and to whom he gave colonization rights in Venezuela (1529-1556). His reign was followed by that of Philip II (1556-1598).

been practiced for some time by the Portuguese crown. However, as time went on, they almost disappeared among the Portuguese, whereas the Spaniards developed and resolutely maintained them. Nonetheless, at that time, it was the Portuguese who established the various norms and characteristics of the slave trade in Africa, Europe, and America. In fact, the Spanish crown frequently had recourse to the knowledge and experience of the Portuguese slave traders. They were specialized not only in the details of the trade itself but in such questions as the demand for slaves in all the different points of America, and in the capacity of each of the trading settlements in Africa to provide the required numbers of slaves.[3]

The system of licenses, with their exclusive trading rights, was in one respect a serious disadvantage for the Spanish colonists. It tended to inflate the cost of slaves, since in practice the licensee did not actually import the Africans himself. He sold the licenses to other merchants and these, in their turn, to yet others until in due course they came into the hands of the Portuguese who monopolized the trade. The result was that a license for which the crown had charged 3 ducats would eventually be worth 8. Later, when the basic price went up to 30, the final price would be 80. And this leaves out of account, in the total price charged to the colonist, such things as food, insurance, transport, and royal taxes.[4]

From 1532 to 1589 the granting of exclusive, monopolistic trading licenses was withdrawn, and commerce in slaves was taken over entirely by the Casa de la Contratación de las Indias and the Consulado of Seville.[5] The main reasons for

[3] Sampaio, 1957.

[4] Aguirre Beltrán, 1946; Saco, 1937-44; and Las Casas, 1951.

[5] The Casa de la Contratación (1503-1790) was established to retain colonial maritime affairs and commerce under direct crown control. It was not in itself a trading entity, since commerce devolved on private capital (cf. the Portuguese Casa da India, which operated trade very much as a crown monopoly). The powers and obligations of the Casa were wide: to collect duties and the royal share of precious metals and stones; to ensure that none but Old Christians migrated, so as to safeguard the Indies against heresy; to form a repository of technical information (standard charts, a school of navigation, the licensing of pilots); to act as trustee for intestate New World colonists; to judge commercial suits, breaches of its rules, and offenses on the high seas. Outbound (in respect to slavery, see chap. 3) and returning fleets sailed between the port of Seville and specified ports in

the change were the high price of slaves, the growing demand, the fact that the crown's policy on the slave trade had become more economically and politically oriented, the increase of smuggling associated with the trade, and the zealous measures adopted by Seville to protect its commercial monopoly. Smuggling had serious consequences for the settlers in Brazil, who needed African slaves to overcome their labor problems. The Portuguese operators in Africa, and the traders who obtained licenses from the Portuguese crown, far preferred to trade with the Spanish colonies, as already mentioned. Various historians have emphasized that the shortage of African slaves in Brazil, at that particular time, was not only due to a lack of coordination in the overall economic policies of the Portuguese crown, but that it was also a straightforward case of commercial convenience. Quite simply, the price that could be obtained for Africans in the Spanish colonies was very much higher and was paid in silver or gold.

The trade developed in a specific way. Licenses for slaves shipped at Angola for Brazil cost only three thousand reis in the way of export duties, whereas those for the Spanish possessions cost twice as much.[6] In practice this meant that nearly all the slaves were ostensibly shipped for Brazil. Some few of them would be dropped there, and the rest taken to Spanish ports in so-called damaged ships. These were ships which, when they approached Spanish coasts, would declare that they were badly damaged, and in this way gain official permission to enter ports that were otherwise forbidden from engaging in international trade.[7] Manifestly, all this could only be carried on with the complicity of Portuguese and

---

the Indies (Cartagena, Portobelo, and Veracruz). See Haring, 1939; and Parry, *The Spanish Seaborne Empire* (London, 1966), pp. 54 ff.

The *consulados* were legally incorporated merchant guilds or chambers of commerce, which, besides being associations, were tribunals in commercial matters involving their members (bankruptcy, contracts, etc.). Appeals were heard by civil courts with the aid of the consulados. The Consulado of Seville, formally established in 1543 (Parry, p. 125), was invested with the monopoly of the New World trade. It handled an extensive commission business on behalf of European merchant houses. The consulados in America in general patterned their articles on those of the Sevillian consulado.

[6] Boxer, 1952; and Goulart, 1949. *Reis* is the plural of *real*, the smaller unit of Portuguese currency.

[7] Goulart, 1949; and Abreu e Brito, 1931.

Spanish officials, since (as the astute Portuguese slave trader Duarte Lopes stressed) the official import duties for the Spanish colonies were very much higher than for the Portuguese ones.[8]

The long period under discussion—most of the sixteenth century—corresponds chronologically to the era of the conquest and rapid Spanish expansion on mainland America. It also corresponds to the time when private capital and private interests were a foremost consideration, especially insofar as the conquistador himself was concerned, given his relative independence and power and his capacity as entrepreneur and encomendero. For the institution of slavery, it corresponds to the time when trading licenses were given as an outright grant by the king, and also when the annuities granted against the seizure of capital, already described, were being paid by the issuance of more permits to import African slaves.

The licenses which the Casa de la Contratación granted in its period of control became so numerous that it is almost impossible to group them in a schematic way.[9] In a very general sense, the individuals and institutions listed below received licenses to transport varying numbers of African slaves, sometimes a thousand or more. The first groups named are the ones who received the least.

1. Royal officials and the clergy, who came to take up appointments in the Indies. Their slaves were granted by free concession, since they were exempt from duties and taxes.[10]

2. The conquistadors and other people considered deserving in the conquest, who received their licenses as compensation for their services and for the expenses they had incurred in the work of conquest and expansion. Such licenses were given by free grant, special agreement, or in payment of annuities.

---

[8] Sampaio, 1957. Duarte Lopes was famous as a traveler in central Africa in the late sixteenth century. He journeyed as far as Lakes Nyasa and Tanganyika. His *Relação do Reino do Congo*, published about 1591, was extremely popular, resulting in a large number of editions and translations.

[9] For an approximate calculation on the number of slaves imported at this time into Spanish America, see chap. 3.

[10] Mellafe, 1959.

3. Some of the local town councils, the *cabildos*, which availed themselves of the trade as an economic investment so as to better secure the financial needs of their institutions. In the technical language of the time, such capital investment was specifically described as forming part of the financial estate or assets of the town. It is worth noting that other public institutions, such as hospitals and convents, also obtained slaves in this way. This practice was not confined to the Spanish and Portuguese possessions in the New World but was common to other parts of their empires, as for example, the Canary Islands.[11] The concessions in all these cases were based on an institutional grant rather than an individual one.

4. Spaniards who had distinguished themselves in some special way in services to the crown, apart from services rendered in the conquest. A number of those who had fought on the king's side in the civil wars in Peru is a case in point.[12]

5. Favorites of the king, or privileged people in the court, the Council of the Indies, or the Casa de la Contratación.

6. Private individuals, merchants, conquistadors, or businessmen who signed particular agreements with the crown. An example would be the articles signed in Madrid in 1580 by the king and Ventura Espino, by which the king conceded all the mines in Peru which were not already leased. Among the subsidiary grants which the crown gave so that the contract could be carried out was the right to import a thousand slaves over a period of six years. They were to be obtained from Cape Verde, São Tomé, or any other convenient place in Guinea or in Brazil.[13]

The Portuguese Period of Slave Contracts

The Casa de la Contratación and the University of Merchants[14] in Seville, zealously concerned to keep direct and

[11] Levillier, 1921, vol. II; and Márquez de la Plata, 1928; and Goulart, 1949.
[12] Mellafe, 1959.
[13] Biblioteca Municipal de Lima, *Cedulario del Cabildo*, vol. II. It is not known whether this agreement was ever actually carried into effect. Other examples can be found in Mellafe, 1959.
[14] "University" is used here in its medieval and sixteenth-century sense of a

absolute control of the slave trade, had their own way for many years. However, a crisis was reached toward the end of the sixteenth century. This was not wholly confined to the slave trade. It was far more the first serious breakdown of the entire commercial system monopolized by Seville, and of the system of annual fleets.[15] If one looks only at slavery, however, there were a number of important contributing causes. It has already been explained that the system prevailing up to that time had brought about a severe price inflation through the sale and resale of licenses. The fact that the principal sources of the supply of slaves were always in the hands of the Portuguese was a significant determining factor. From 1580, when the crowns of Portugal and Spain became united under Philip II, there seemed to be no serious political reason to exclude the Portuguese merchants from the monopoly of the trade, and from allowing them some access to the Indies. It was considered as a possible, partial solution to the problem of transport and delays in the delivery of slaves to the New World, where they were in extreme demand. What is more, it was expected that a possible saturation of the market would bring down prices.

On the other hand, Philip II and the Council of the Indies had many years previously initiated a policy of separating as far as possible the affairs of state from the private sector and private interests which had been so important in the conquest. A means to this end was gradual reduction in the granting of licenses as a free concession. Nonetheless, a little before the first *asiento* was given to the Portuguese, there was a backlog of licenses for some six thousand slaves which had been granted to individuals but not yet delivered to the New World.

The first asiento, or contract which gave the Portuguese exclusive rights, was signed in 1595, between the crown and Pedro Gomes Reynel. He was to arrange to supply 4,250 African slaves a year until he had imported a total of 38,250. The slaves could be obtained from any source but could enter

professional association or guild. It was particularly applied to merchants, denoting aspects of association, whereas "consulado" implied also a capacity to act as a tribunal, though the same body was and is frequently referred to by both terms.

[15] H. and P. Chaunu, 1956-59, vol. VIII.

America only through the port of Cartagena. From there Gomes Reynel's representatives could travel to all the Spanish provinces except Tierra Firme (present-day Venezuela and northern Colombia); there were restrictions on the numbers of slaves for Buenos Aires.[16] Gomes Reynel was to pay the crown 900,000 ducats for these rights, in installments of 100,000 ducats a year for the nine years of the contract. Before this contract ran out, another was signed in 1601 with João Rodrigues Coutinho; in 1605, because of his death, it was transferred to his brother, Gonzalo Vaz. In 1615 António Rodrigues de Elvas obtained the contract. Manuel Rodrigues Lamego followed in 1623. The final one granted to the Portuguese was signed in 1631 with Melchor Gomes Angel and Cristóvão Mendes de Sousa. This lasted until 1640.[17]

The general conditions stipulated by all these asientos were more or less the same. There was always the embargo on Tierra Firme and the restrictions for Buenos Aires. In 1615, Veracruz was added as a second port of entry. The Spanish crown never surrendered the right to specify precisely the points of entry, the provinces where the Africans could be sold, and the numbers that could be taken to each region. However, the agents of the different contractors had certain preferences which were naturally related to the degree of demand in different places and the ease of access to these places. Such preferences were for the Antilles, Mexico, and the Atlantic coast of Venezuela and Colombia. The result of their operations in these particular areas was a temporary saturation of the market and a decided drop in prices.

In notable contrast, there were many places in the colonial empire still largely untouched by these operations. The deficient supply in South America was largely brought about by its having to pass through Panama, entailing as it did special permits, higher costs, and greater risks. It is not surprising that Ecuador, Peru, Upper Peru (present-day Bolivia), Tucumán, the River Plate region, and Chile demanded a more regular supply. Since it was not forthcoming legally, they had recourse to smuggling, which was organized

[16] Only one lot of 600 slaves was to be allowed to be taken to Buenos Aires. See Mellafe, 1959; and Veitia Linage, 1945.

[17] Molinari, 1916.

on a grand scale in the Rio de La Plata, using links with various Brazilian ports. Smuggling was in fact one of the reasons for the termination of asientos to the Portuguese, and the beginning of a new era in the slave trade. Nonetheless, it was not the sole reason, or even the most important. In 1599 the island of São Tomé fell into Dutch hands. From then on, the Portuguese gradually lost their best possessions in Africa and with them the monopoly of the slave trade. Thus a number of contractors, Gomes Reynel and others, suffered severe financial losses when they were unable to compete with the Dutch trade in contraband African slaves.[18] The year 1640 marks the end of the asiento granted to Gomes Angel and Mendes de Sousa, and likewise the end of the supremacy of the Portuguese in the slave trade. It is no mere coincidence that it also marks the separation anew of the crowns of Portugal and Spain.

International Competition and the Return to the Asiento System

The period from 1640 to 1692 was a confused time. Spain's control of its share of the slave trade was often vacillating and weak—perhaps the direct result of the economic decline which Spain and its empire were undergoing. There are a number of specific characteristics of the period which are fundamental to the slave trade. International competition in particular was becoming more intense. There was increasing rivalry among the mercantile powers for supremacy overseas, and the African slave trade had become one of its most important issues. Apart from being a business venture in its own right, it also constituted an excellent means of economic penetration into the American continent. Slaves could be smuggled in, and in return all sorts of goods in strong demand in Europe, besides precious metals, could be brought back. One can well understand the central importance the slave trade came to assume in European, rather than merely Spanish and Portuguese, politics and diplomatic life. It became a major consideration of ambassadors, and of alliances and treaties.

[18] Aguirre Beltrán, 1946; Saco, 1937-44; and Mellafe, 1959.

The Spanish crown, increasingly weaker and under pressure from the new expansionist powers, found itself caught in a vicious circle from which it was never able to escape. If it suspended trade in slaves, as it attempted to do between 1640 and 1651, the American market would have to rely on smuggled ones. The colonies could then well complain of the indifference of the home power to their problems and plight. On the other hand, to allow the trade to continue implied the giving of concessions to old enemies, and the gradual loss of exclusive rights and monopolies. It even represented a compromise of revered, traditional religious principles, which had been one of the motivating forces behind the formation of Spain's empire, her period of political supremacy in Europe, and, in fact, behind a whole century of enormous expenses and interminable wars. Spain was at a severe disadvantage in that it was almost the only one among the European powers of that time which had no slaving stations in Africa. Its former union with Portugal degenerated into a state of war in 1640. It was not until 1668 that Portugal gained definitive recognition of its independence. The conflict between Spain and its traditional supplier of slaves was a golden opportunity for Holland to take over the trade directly or indirectly. As one of its results, the Dutch were able to acquire a share in shipping slaves from Europe to the Indies. Because of its economic crisis, Spain was not able to maintain sufficient serviceable vessels for this purpose.

The situation was very little to the liking of the officials and merchants of either Spain or Portugal. The two kingdoms, caught in a dilemma by the competition of more powerful nations, had a good deal to lose in the way of colonial commerce and economic independence. A major part of the clandestine trade in slaves was carried on through Brazil. This meant that at least the Portuguese slave traders of the West African port of Cacheu had the opportunity to keep some of the trade with the Spanish colonies. The Portuguese crown itself, in order to salvage something of the most lucrative part of its overseas trade, in 1647 allowed Spanish traders direct access to the purchase of slaves in Guinea, despite the fact that at the time Spain and Portugal were in a state of war.[19] The Portuguese were tenacious in their struggle to hold their position in the trade. This explains their recovery in 1696 when the company of Cacheu and Cape Verde gained, although only temporarily, the monopoly of the trade with the Spanish empire.

From 1651 to 1662, the University of Merchants in Seville directly controlled the commerce in slaves with the Spanish possessions. It faced strong opposition from the Casa de la Contratación and from various groups of merchants and companies who had greatly profited from the comparatively free trade and the smuggling of preceding years. In this period (1651-1662), and also in the years immediately preceding 1676, when the University of Merchants again had responsibility for the trade, disorganization, administrative fees, and excessive taxes came to their peak. The Consulado of Seville was joined by other merchant guilds in America, especially the Consulado of Lima. These consulados together came to constitute the last stronghold of a closed monopoly, with specified ports of entry, a commercial blockade of the Plata region, and the dominance of Peru in the affairs of South American trade.[20] For its part, the crown had some years previously leased to the consulados the right to collect a whole series of taxes, some of which were directly concerned with the importation of Negro slaves. It is especially on this account that the consulados were interested in keeping a close watch on, if not firm control of, the various aspects of the trade. There later arose numerous severe disagreements with *asentistas*, those traders who had signed slaving contracts with the crown.

The shortage of shipping and of direct sources for the supply of African slaves were the main causes bringing about a return to the former system of asientos, with exclusive, monopolistic trading rights granted to a single trader or company. In 1662 a contract was concluded with the Genoese merchants, Domingo Grillo and Ambrosio and Agustín Lomelín. This was known as the Asiento of the Grillos. It was renewed for a further term in 1668, despite the fact that

[19] Goulart, 1949.
[20] Scelle, 1906; Scheuss de Studer, 1958; Aguirre Beltrán, 1946; Céspedes del Castillo, 1947; Rodríguez, 1956; and Boxer, 1957.

the Genoese had to turn to the Dutch in order to complete the conditions of their contract. It was also alleged that they had become deeply implicated in smuggling, in not declaring their true earnings, and in not paying all the dues owed by them to the crown. Subsequently, similar asientos were granted to Antonio García and Sebastián Siliceo in 1674, and to Juan Barroso del Pozo in 1679 and 1682. The 1682 asiento included a partner Nicolás Porcio who was closely associated with the Dutch companies which operated in Africa. Because of this, when Juan Barroso died, he was replaced in the contract by Balthasar Coymans, who was an associate and agent of the West India Company of Amsterdam. Dutch influence reached its peak in 1689 when Porcio and Coymans managed to obtain an extension of their contract for a further five years.

In the meantime, the slave trade had undergone a number of important technical modifications. The new asientos stipulated annual quotas which fluctuated in numbers between 3,500 and 6,000 *piezas* to be supplied to the Spanish colonies.[21] The asentistas were required by the crown to pay both the usual taxes, which were collected by royal officials or the consulados, and also the fees payable as a result of the acquisition of the asiento itself. The method of paying against the issuance of a license, current up to this point, proved administratively inconvenient in the altered circumstances. Thus concessions began to be granted which specified payment against "tonnage" of African slaves, that is to say, slaves calculated against ship's tonnage rather than on a basis of a per capita license system. This is significant in that officially a ton was considered to correspond to three Negroes, whereas in practice it would include up to seven. It represented the beginning of incredible overcrowding in

---

[21] The pieza system was an attempt to measure slaves in terms of quality rather than merely by number; that is, in terms of their potential as laborers. A full *pieza de Indias* was a slave who met certain defined specifications of age, physical condition, size, and health; otherwise, slaves were considered as parts of a pieza; that is, the actual numbers of slaves imported under an asiento was normally higher than the corresponding pieza numbers. The contract of the Cacheu Company (1696-1703; see p. 52, below), for example, stipulated 4,000 slaves a year who were to form 2,500 piezas. See Scelle, 1906, vol. II, pp. 26-27; and Curtin, 1969, pp. 22-23.

the holds of slave ships, with an ensuing high death rate, and the practice of all kinds of frauds.[22]

The main ports of entry for these cargoes were Portobelo, Cartagena, Havana, Veracruz, and Campeche. However, the agents of the asentistas traveled to almost all the provinces in Spanish America. The contractors gradually secured terms which were more and more favorable. They were allowed to transport their cargoes in ships of foreign manufacture. They were no longer obliged to obtain their slaves from specific regions in Africa. Eventually they were even permitted by the crown to acquire their slaves in Curaçao and Jamaica, which were used as storage areas for slaves and as centers for contraband trade with the Spanish possessions in the Antilles, Central America, Venezuela, and Colombia.[23]

The Role of Commercial Companies

Throughout the seventeenth century Portugal, France, England, and Holland developed their overseas empires largely by means of commercial companies. It was inevitable that, sooner or later, they should come to challenge the absolute hold of Spain on her empire in America, while at the same time assuring themselves of a commercial monopoly and political authority in the remaining continents. The slave trade had become highly complex and costly at the same time that the Spanish empire deteriorated economically. The trade had come to demand a capital investment which could only be made by commercial companies with their much greater concentration of financial resources. Spain certainly could no longer finance or control the slave trade, and the task became largely the private responsibility and risk of the asentista himself, evidenced by the fact that several of the slave traders mentioned were forced into bankruptcy.

On the appearance of the big commercial companies, it is perhaps pertinent to make one or two general observations. It is evident that the African slave trade on the one hand, and the slave as a means of production on the other, could

---

[22] A ship's "ton" (*tonelada*) was roughly equivalent at the time to 2.8 cubic meters capacity. For the implications of this on the calculation of the number of slaves transshipped, see pp. 70-71 ff., above; and Curtin, 1969.

[23] Saco, 1937-44; Scelle, 1906; and Scheuss de Studer, 1958.

not be separated. In the evolution of capitalism, they could be said to be part and parcel of a developing commercialism in the economic sense, and of absolutism in the political sense. However, as the slave trade became increasingly the object of the political maneuvering of European powers, so it became more and more dissociated from the requirements of production in the New World. Thus the commercial inflow of slaves, the numbers available, and the quotas fixed by the home authorities for each region of the continent often bore little or no relation to the needs of these regions. Good cases were Brazil, the Viceroyalty of Peru, and the region of La Plata, all of which for two centuries regularly made demands for slaves which were never fully met. Problems created by abolition movements and the insistence on introducing slaves into regions where their work was virtually unproductive are matters that will be examined later. In any case, the gap existing between the trade as such and an economy that required slavery for effective production is quite evident. The creation of large companies was obviously far more closely associated with the trade itself and the movement of capital in Europe than with a precise type of production. The European powers seem to have found it more convenient to engage in political negotiations over the trade if it happened to be concentrated in the hands of only one or two big companies. The European monarchs, the Phillips of Spain, Louis XIV of France, Queen Anne of England, and Pedro II of Portugal, thus became business associates and promoters in the slave trade when they fostered and contributed financially to these companies.[24] As far as the individual countries are concerned, the take-over of the trade by the various companies was facilitated by differing factors. For Spain it was closely related to a last attempt to preserve its commercial monopoly in its American empire. For Portugal it was associated with an effort to recover something of its former place in the trade. For France, it was part of its influence in Spanish politics at the beginning of the eighteenth century.[25]

[24] Acosta Saignes, 1961a.

[25] Other ideas from both similar and different points of view on the place of slavery in the evolution of capitalism can be found in such works as Cardoso, 1962; Conrad and Meyers, 1964; Davis, 1966; Foner and Genovese, 1969; Weinstein and Gattel, 1968; and Williams, 1964 and 1970.

Dutch supremacy in the slave trade came to an end in 1694, when an asiento was signed with Bernardo Francisco Marín de Guzmán. He was a merchant of Caracas, who had extensive business connections in Seville and Lisbon. The Spanish crown was particularly enthusiastic about the idea that the asiento was to be managed in the Indies. They saw in it the opportunity to recoup something of their old autonomy in the trade, and to curb smuggling. However, Marín de Guzmán planned to carry out his contract through Portuguese middlemen operating from the Portuguese African possessions. To this end he began to negotiate with what was known as the Cacheu Company. However, he died before the terms of the contract could be fulfilled. The Cacheu Company applied for the contract, alleging that they had already entered into agreements with Marín de Guzmán. In this way, the Portuguese regained the monopoly of the trade with America from 1696 to 1703.

Although the Portuguese crown, the Portuguese slave traders in Africa, and the merchants who operated in Brazil would all have liked to continue the slave trade with the Spanish possessions, in fact it was by now no longer feasible. Even their smuggling trade had almost completely disappeared. The main reason was the complete change in circumstances in Brazil at the beginning of the eighteenth century. It had ceased to be secondary in the overall colonial policy of the Portuguese crown. Gold mining in Minas Gerais, Cuiabá, Goiás, and Bahia (Salvador) was developing apace, and so was tropical agriculture.[26] They were absorbing all the slaves they could obtain. The sources of supply which still remained to the Portuguese in Africa, or which they were regaining, became geared to serve the new Brazilian economy. This situation was a radical change from what had prevailed earlier. Previously, if a producer in Brazil had badly needed slaves, he had to go to Africa to get them.

---

[26] Gold was discovered almost simultaneously in different places in Minas Gerais in the period 1693-95; in Cuiabá in 1718; and Goias in 1725. Gold had been found at the beginning of the eighteenth century in the province of Bahia (for some twenty years officially the finds were not supposed to be worked out of fear of attracting foreign attack and of displacing slaves from sugar and tobacco production). They were followed by other finds in 1727, initially administered by Bahia, but later by Minas Gerais. See Boxer, 1969, pp. 35 ff., 267 ff., and 153 ff.

This meant obtaining licenses in the face of the complete lack of interest on the part of the colonial authorities and the crown itself, and getting around the indifference of the Portuguese traders in Africa, who far preferred to keep their best cargoes for the Spanish colonies.

In the seventeenth century some Portuguese traders had gained licenses of relative importance to ship a certain annual number of slaves to particular places or provinces in Brazil. Such traders were, for example, José Erdovico, for 700 Africans for Pará and Maranhão, and Pascoal Pereira Jansen who gained a license in 1682 for a similar number for the same areas. Some small companies, like the Estanco Company, were also concerned. So were some of the larger ones, such as the Cacheu Company. However, these companies had regarded Brazil as only a small part of their business. If it is correct to term these licenses asientos, as some specialists in the field have done, they were very limited in scope, and involved far less in the way of slaves and capital investment than did the Spanish asientos. Eventually Brazil too turned to the commercial companies for the slaves it needed for its economic boom. These companies were either English or Dutch or were formed within the Portuguese empire utilizing Brazilian capital, such as the Grão Pará Company (1755) or the General Trading Company of Pernambuco and Paraíba (1759). At the same time, a part of the supply of slaves was also provided by smuggling, something which had affected Brazil very little previously. Smuggling became a flourishing trade, with payment being made in precious metals. It was operated by the same countries which handled the legal trade through the commercial companies. It was conducted both at the sources of supply in Africa and on the coasts of Portuguese America.[27]

The slave trade would never again be dissociated from the political vicissitudes of Europe—from its alliances, truces, and wars. Spain never recovered its maritime power, so that it was increasingly clear that whoever dominated the seas controlled overseas trade, particularly commerce in slaves. The change of royal houses in Spain also had significant

---

[27] Boxer, 1969a and 1969c; and Goulart, 1949.

economic consequences.[28] From the final decades of the seventeenth century, the king of France, Louis XIV, had been fostering a policy of political supremacy and expansion. This had as one of its results the War of the Spanish Succession (1701-1713). Louis' support for his grandson, later Philip V of Spain, increased French influence in Spain's commercial relations with its empire, and specifically in the slave trade. At the same time, England took advantage of the war to penetrate economically into Spanish America, displacing both its ally, Holland, and its enemy, France.[29] French dominance in the slave trade is exemplified by the concession which Spain granted to the Royal French Guinea Company in 1701 for 4,800 slaves a year for ten years. The conditions of the contract showed the manifest state of bankruptcy of the royal treasury in Spain: the king merely had a token share in the company. He contributed nothing in the way of financing, but instead had to pay an annual rate of interest of 8 percent, which was to be deducted from the dues the company handed over to the treasury. The ships and their crews could be French or Spanish. They could go to almost wherever they wished in Spanish America, even to Buenos Aires and to Callao in Peru, which had hitherto been carefully excluded from such contracts.[30] Despite these extremely favorable terms, the company was not able to keep its side of the contract and was forced to declare bankrupcy in 1710. The precise causes are very complex. In fact they are almost inexplicable if one bears in mind that the French balanced out any losses incurred in legal commerce in Africans by smuggling, or by a return trade from America. Rights to the return trade were often conceded by royal license, and even when they were not, it could be conducted under cover of the slave trade. Moreover, the market for slaves was as good as it ever was. It was seemingly inexhaustible.

Again the explanation is not to be found in any crisis within the trade, but far more in the overall political and financial situation of the time. In the final years of the seventeenth century, a large part of Spanish America suffered commercial

[28] J. H. Parry, *Spanish Seaborne Empire*, 1966.
[29] J. B. Wolf, 1951.
[30] Calvo, 1862, vol. II; Scheuss de Studer, 1958.

depression. In some places, like Peru, it was made worse by a crisis in the agricultural and mining industries. The wars in Europe cut the normal trade between the homeland and the colonies. During the governorship of Viceroy Monclova in Peru (1689-1705), only two commercial fleets reached the Pacific coasts of South America. Meanwhile, hopes for a solution to the crisis were centered in importing more African slaves. Only a very small supply was maintained by smuggling through Paraguay, the River Plate region, Chile, and along the Peruvian coast. By the time the situation began to normalize itself, between 1730 and 1740, the French had lost the opportunity which there had been of developing smuggling on a large scale in South America.[31] If France established a foothold for itself in Spanish American trade in the early years of the century, it certainly had not been able to follow it up politically or in successfully monopolizing the trade. The Royal French Guinea Company, as could perhaps be expected from its name, intended to obtain its slaves from Guinea. However, that territory could not provide a sufficient number of slaves to supply America. The company was forced, then, to seek an annulment of one of the conditions of its contract, which stipulated that the slaves could not be obtained from Costa da Mina or Cape Verde, then controlled by the Dutch and English. When the clause was waived in 1706, it was already too late to avoid bankruptcy and the final victory of England, France's political enemy.

England, despite the war, blockades, and pacts, was involved in general commerce and the slave trade with America, as it had been for the last century. For some years before the restoration of peace in Europe with the Treaty of Utrecht (1713), the English had been trying to obtain from the Spanish crown legal recognition of their role in the Indies trade. Even without the help of its allies, Holland and Portugal, England was in a manifestly strong position to do so. It had the maritime capacity, capital, possessions in Africa, and ports in America essential to the maintenance of an adequate supply of Negro slaves to the continent.

[31] Moreyra Paz-Soldán and Céspedes del Castillo, 1954-55, vol. I; Martin, 1931; and Vignols, 1929.

Negotiations undertaken in 1706 failed, and an appropiate opportunity did not present itself again until 1712, at the end of the long war. Talks held then in Madrid resulted in a number of initial agreements: a treaty giving asiento rights, signed on March 23, 1713; a preliminary treaty establishing peace and a treaty dealing with general commerce. All these were ratified some months later in Utrecht.

England had won a valuable victory. France was no longer a serious competitor in commerce with Spanish America: England took over its recent monopoly of the slave trade, and thereby the opportunity to further its economic penetration of the New World without recourse to smuggling. England also gained rights of free and direct navigation, and in assigned places in Spanish America the right to establish its trading posts.[32] The English crown assigned its asiento to the South Sea Company with the understanding that the company was to take upon itself part of the national debt. Various English bankers and financiers of the time floated the company with great enthusiasm. It reached its maximum prosperity about 1719.

The monopoly gained by the South Sea Company was for 144,000 piezas over a period of 25 years. In order to obtain so many Africans, the company had to sign an agreement with the Royal African Company, which had useful associations with non-English trading posts on the African continent.[33] The points of entry in Spanish America were Campeche, Veracruz, Havana, Cartagena, Portobelo, Panama, Caracas, and Buenos Aires. Through Panama the traders could reach the ports of the Pacific seaboard, although after the Treaty of Madrid (1721), direct access also was granted to Upper Peru (Bolivia), and Chile.[34] Storgage centers, where the slaves were received and from where they were distributed, were set up on the islands of Barbados and Jamaica—the islands which had been hitherto so important for England's clandestine commerce.

[32] Saco, 1937-44; Scheuss de Studer, 1958; MacLachlan, 1940; and Ramsay, 1957.
[33] Davies, 1970, is a very useful work on the South Sea Company, its organization, its relations with other English companies, and the efforts and connections made by some of the latter to become associated with the asiento.
[34] Calvo, 1862, vol. II; Saco, 1937-44; and Acosta Saignes, 1961.

Although England had formally ousted her old competitors from legal commerce with Spanish America, in practice it was virtually impossible to prevent them from trading. The French engaged in contraband. The Dutch traded between Curaçao and the coasts of Venezuela. The Portuguese, operating from Brazil and the colony of Sacramento, posed serious competition in the southern half of the continent.[35]

The South Sea Company itself had other grave problems. It had difficulties with its shareholders, with the English crown, with other English companies, and with shipping interests in Bristol and Liverpool. The peace of 1713 and the various treaties which had been signed then were not lasting. Spain and England became involved in open hostilities in 1718, 1727, and 1739. During these times the company's agencies in Spanish American ports were abandoned or confiscated. There was also the hostility of local officials, and the attacks of Spanish pirates on the company's slave vessels. The company had direct responsibility in the events that led to the war of 1739. In addition, it had not paid slave duties to the Spanish treasury or the share of trading profits owing to the king. For his part, the Spanish monarch had not paid the company certain sums owed it. The two sides had differing views on the expiration of the term of the asiento and its possible renewal.[36]

Development of Free Trade

The opening up of the slave trade to free commerce was not a sudden, unexpected change in the economic policies of the Iberian powers. It was one that had been made inevitable over a long period of time by the gradually changing circumstances of colonial production and trade. In the case of Spain it was part of the effort of Charles III and

[35] The colony of Sacramento (see map 3) was established by the Portuguese (1680) to secure access to the Rio de la Plata; as a countermeasure, Montevideo was founded by the Spaniards in 1726. Imprecise demarcation of the border resulted in frequent military hostilities and diplomatic negotiations. The Treaty of Madrid (1750) attempted a solution, but it was not definitive until the Treaty of San Ildefonso (1777). In these treaties Sacramento was assigned to Spain in return for other concessions.

[36] Scheuss de Studer, 1958; and Davies, 1970.

his ministers to reorganize old colonial structures.[37] Up to this point the slave trade had developed as an economic element which was largely independent and distinct from the rest of the commerce conducted between Spain and her colonies. However, the freedom of trade which was now evolving in the history of African slavery was far from being an isolated commercial phenomenon. Apart from this, there are other points to be considered. The South Sea Company had suffered the same problems which had bankrupted nearly all the other companies that had signed asiento agreements with the Spanish crown. But it had further difficulties with the House of Commons and with the shipowners of Bristol and Liverpool. The consequence was that before the expiration of its asiento, England had to allow freedom of trade in slaves to her subjects, who as a matter of fact already controlled a large part of the commerce between Africa and America. England had developed the slave trade to a high level of commercial sophistication by means of its large companies, but when they became uneconomic and restrictive the only recourse was free trade. Spain and Portugal were at the time involved in experimenting with the system of companies, but it was many years before they imitated England by turning to a more open system of trade.

The commercial dependence of Spain and Portugal on England became increasingly obvious as the eighteenth century progressed. There was no question of competing with the control that England had of large markets, maritime transport, and the mobilization of capital. The English had the capacity of making quick, efficient changes in their commercial policies as circumstances warranted, while other

---

[37] Charles III (1716-1788) of the Bourbons (he reigned from 1759), with very definite ideas on kingship and strongly motivated by the desire to make Spain and its empire internally and externally strong, is often cited as an example of enlightened despotism. This is perhaps well epitomized by his expulsion of approximately 3,000 Jesuits from the New World in 1767. The decree gave no reasons and enjoined silence, Charles adding that "it was not for them (his vassals) to judge or interpret the commands of their sovereign." In many ways he achieved his goals, despite international reverses (e.g., the war with England, 1762) and perhaps sometimes his not having gone far enough. He extensively rationalized administration, taxes, defense, communications (especially in the present context, new routes and ports), administrative boundaries in the empire, agencies of local government, and education.

nations could only achieve similar results after vacillation and guesswork. Portugal was in a particularly complex situation. It was more dependent on England than Spain was. A contributing factor was that from the sixteenth century it had, in a sense, combined free trade with monopolies operated by commercial companies. In an attempt to counteract Portugal's growing dependence on England in the eighteenth century, the Marquis of Pombal promoted state sanctioned slave trading monopolies at a time when free trade was developing as a major new economic possibility.[38]

The 1739 war with England caused the Spanish crown to grant a number of asientos in order to supply its colonial market. However, they were limited agreements which did not imply trading rights on a large monopolistic scale, and they were signed with individuals rather than companies. Nonetheless, these concessions were a departure from the monopoly that the South Sea Company had been given, although generally the Spanish merchants who were granted them had to go to the agents of this or some other English company. Eventually, the various concessions and monopolies given to the South Sea Company were legally concluded in 1750, when the Treaty of the Palacio del Buen Retiro was signed.[39] Meanwhile, the return to the traditional system of limited concessions resolved nothing. The old bureaucratic complications appeared anew. Clandestine trade in slaves, fostered by the Spanish asentistas themselves and Spanish colonial officials, which utilized the old, well-established routes and bases, became more of a major problem than ever before.

[38] The Marquis de Pombal (Sebastião José de Carvalho e Mello, 1699-1782) was noted for his combination of ruthlessness and desire for reform. On the accession of José I (1750) he was appointed secretary for war and foreign affairs, and served as chief minister from 1756 to the end of José's reign (1777). Pombal reviewed finances, the army, education, industry, and commerce, especially the establishment of commercial companies to foster foreign trade. The port wine monopoly had provoked riots in Oporto, which he subsequently drastically punished. He also investigated the size of landed estates and the power of the nobles. He expelled the Jesuits from Portugal and its dominations in 1759; attempted a more unified and rational system of colonial administration; and was more than energetic in advancing Portuguese territorial claims in colonial boundary disputes with Spain (see n. 35 above).

[39] MacLachlan, 1940; and Saco, 1937-44.

Renewed war with England in 1762, which especially affected the Spanish colonial possessions, accelerated change in slave trade policies. The capture of Havana by England and the subsequent opening of Cuba to free trade during the short period of English control was considered a worthwhile experience by the local authorities and producers. From then on they did whatever they could to secure free trade on a more permanent basis. They did not achieve complete freedom of commerce in the slave trade until 1789. Until then, there existed side by side the mutually antagonistic elements of a gradually developing free trade on the one hand, and asientos with more or less exclusive rights on the other, at least in respect to some provinces in the Indies.[40]

From 1760 to 1772, for example, Miguel Uriarte of Cádiz, with a number of Basque associates, had a contract to import three thousand slaves a year through Cartagena, Portobelo, Campeche, Honduras, and a number of minor Caribbean ports. In mid-1772, Uriarte and his partners declared bankruptcy. The maximum selling price of their slaves had been fixed, and heavy import duties imposed. Other similar contracts were subsequently granted, but they were even more restrictive and limited. In 1773, it was the Sociedad Aguirre y Arístegui (the General Company of Negroes), and in 1785, Edward Barry with the help of capital from New Spain. In 1786, Peter Baker and John Dawson, shipowners from Liverpool, were granted a like concession.[41]

Signs of the imminence of free trade occurred immediately after the 1762 war. The uncertain state of communications between Spain and its colonies resulted in the establishment of the so-called system of mailboats, which had free access with their goods to many ports. In 1765, a complex series of taxes and duties, imposed as a means of customs control and as a safeguard for traditional closed monopolies protected by the state, were abolished. Their abolition, and the inclusion of other major Peninsular ports besides Cádiz and Seville in Caribbean trade, greatly facilitated Spanish commerce. The efforts of Charles III to initiate a policy of

[40] King, 1942; Saco, 1937-44; Scheuss de Studer, 1958; and Acosta Saignes, 1961a.
[41] Acosta Saignes, 1961a.

commercial reform, which had begun in a hesitant and tentative way in the mid-century years, became fully implemented in the final three decades of the century. The free trade regulations of 1778 were fundamental to the reform, as they extended the concessions to all the Spanish American provinces except Venezuela, Cumaná, Guayana, and Maracaibo.

The low level of agricultural, mining, and semi-industrial production in Spain's American possessions at the time was regularly attributed to a shortage of labor, and invariably the solution put forward was more African slaves at cheaper prices. This was one of the reasons for the action of Charles III and his ministers in trying to change the situation. A further step was the Treaty of Commerce and Friendship signed by Spain and Portugal in 1778. Spain obtained the African islands of Fernando Póo and Annobón, and the right of direct access for her slave-traders to the remaining Portuguese possessions in Africa in order to acquire Negro slaves. It was a serious, though by now an over-tardy, attempt to gain some independence from the foreign powers which had always controlled Spain's sources of supply in Africa. But such small possessions could not accomplish much, and Spanish merchants and companies had to continue to buy their Africans from the Portuguese, French, Dutch, and English.

An additional step towards liberalization of the Spanish slave trade was taken when hostilities were renewed with England in 1779. The English privateers disrupted the flow of Africans who were now being shipped by Spaniards to their American markets. The result was that the authorities allowed any Spanish subject to import slaves from Spain or from any neutral power during the period of the war. Some provinces were excluded from this concession: La Plata, Chile, and Peru. For these regions the drain of currency and precious metals overseas brought about by smuggling remained as serious a problem as ever.[42] Despite the fact that at the end of the war in 1783 the importation of slaves reverted to what it had been previously, a favorable atmo-

[42] King, 1942; and Scheuss de Studer, 1958.

sphere had nonetheless been created for the complete freedom of international trade. Also commerce was made easier by fixing a single maximum price at which the slaves could be sold, and by reducing the import duty to 6 percent of this price.[43]

From this point on the pressure for completely free trade increased apace. Furthermore, the ministers, José de Gálvez and then Floridablanca, were themselves inclined to favor it.[44] Added to this was the failure of the Philippine Company, which clearly showed once more that Spanish capital and companies alone had severe limitations. Also, the contract which had been granted to Baker and Dawson, who had been assigned the districts of Havana and Caracas, came to an end. Eventually, Floridablanca, in 1789, when Charles IV was king, decreed freedom of trade in African slaves for the provinces of Caracas, Cuba, Santo Domingo, and Puerto Rico. This was the first breach. In 1791 the viceroyalties of Santa Fe and Buenos Aires were added. The following year permission was granted for slave vessels to remain up to forty days in Spanish American ports. In 1793, Spain's American subjects were allowed to go themselves for slaves directly to Africa, and to pay for them with their own products without having to pay duties. The Viceroyalty of Peru received all these concessions in 1795, the ports of Paita and Callao being authorized for the purpose. The permission given to Peru, La Plata, including former Upper Peru, and the Captaincy General of Chile was limited to periods of two, three, or four years, but extensions were granted in 1798,

[43] Biblioteca Nacional de Lima, MSS. C. 1014, C. 1033, and C. 1460.

[44] José de Gálvez, first as inspector-general in Mexico (1765-71) and later as minister of the Indies (from 1775), was responsible for extensive administrative reorganization in Spanish America, especially in attempting to close the gap between viceregal and local administrations (by the intendency system, *intendencias*, with provincial administrators who exercised wide powers). It was on his orders that Upper California was occupied (1769).

The Count of Floridablanca was closely associated with the reform policies of Charles III. He was made first secretary of state in 1776 and served in a highly efficient way up to 1792, three years after the accession of Charles IV. It was at his suggestion that a cabinet of ministers of departmental heads was established (1787) rather than a confused network of councils. The French Revolution had a profound effect on his attitudes, turning him against some of the achievements of his earlier years.

1800, and 1804. By 1804 all the major ports of Spanish America had rights of complete freedom of trade in African slaves.[45]

At the beginning of the nineteenth century, the slave trade, as a free form of commerce, suffered vicissitudes which, at times, brought it to a standstill. The war with England in 1804, and the beginning of the abolition movement in the English slave trade in 1807, were of direct consequence to the supply of slaves to America. From 1810, when Spanish American independence movements began, and during the ensuing fighting, the slave trade almost completely halted. However, this did not imply the extinction of the trade or the immediate abolition of slavery.

[45] King, 1942; Scheuss de Studer, 1958; Diaz Soler, 1953; *Documentos para la historia argentina*, 1916, vol. VII; and Biblioteca Nacional de Lima, MS. D.9634.

CHAPTER THREE

SOURCES, ROUTES,
AND MARKETING OF SLAVES

African Sources of Slaves

The first two chapters have surveyed the history of the slave trade from a general political and economic point of view. The present chapter will examine those factors that characterized the trade within the economic structure of the Spanish empire. In this sense there are two basic points worth bearing in mind. First, the importation of African slaves involved two different stages: transshipment from African coasts to authorized ports of intake in America and distribution from these points of entry to the various parts of Spanish America. It should already be clear that it was only rarely and under specifically controlled conditions that those involved in shipping the slaves were also allowed to market them at their eventual points of destination. Transshipment necessitated royal permission, customs duties, and registers, access to one or more sources of supply in Africa, vessels, and extensive capital resources. Distribution implied an established internal commercial network, commercial agents, traders, local middlemen, and regional economic activities requiring labor. Second is the clandestine commerce in slaves, which makes it impossible to analyse completely all aspects of the trade. Perhaps we will never know exactly how many slave ships and slaves came to America, or the precise internal organization or routes involved.

When the trade was in its comparative infancy, slave ships that left for the New World would do so as part of the fleets from Seville to the Indies. However, it was expensive and risky to hold large numbers of slaves, obtained directly from Africa, in Spanish ports awaiting the necessary maritime connection in order to sail to the New World. The result was that slave ships gained a certain autonomy in being allowed to sail independently of the fleets. They were in fact called ships outside the fleets. This is one point that distinguishes the slave trade from general commerce carried out with the New World. In the course of the seventeenth century, frequent economic crises, especially the shortage of Spanish sea transport and the economic and political pressures imposed by other European powers, caused the trade to move more and more out of the control of the Casa de la Contratación in Seville. The consequence was that the most usual route became the direct one from the African seaboard to such entry ports as Cartagena, Veracruz, or Havana, or to some of the islands which the English, Dutch, and French used as storage and distribution centers, such as Barbados, Curaçao, and Jamaica. Up to the middle of the seventeenth century, the Canary Islands were frequently used as a resupply point for Spanish and Portuguese slavers.

The African ports or the places where the slaves originated or were transported from are very important, not merely for the sake of curiosity but because they help one to understand some of the cultural characteristics introduced by the slaves into America and to explain some of the Latin American racial heritage. The Spaniards had the practice of declaring what country, or what *casta* or stock, the various shipments of slaves came from. If a slave had been shipped from, acquired in, or born in Guinea, for example, the appropriate documents would describe him as Guinean by casta or by country. This custom has been of great help in contemporary research. The reason for the designations on the part of the Spanish authorities was that some types of slaves were said to have certain advantages or disadvantages. Some were not allowed to be taken to America at all. In practice, however, the traders and middlemen often confused the places of origin with those of embarkation or where they were kept awaiting shipment.[1]

A clear picture of the places of origin can be pieced together from an examination of the declarations and lists made by slave traders, the points of embarkation, and the general development of the trade.[2] They fall into a number of zones which progressively replace each other in comparative importance, starting in the north and moving gradually southward down the African continent. Six such zones can be distinguished (see map 4).

1. The first was the North African or Mauritanian region and would include the Canary Islands in the north and extend to the border of modern Senegal and the coast of Cape Verde. The Canary Islands were used mainly as a storage center and a convenient staging point for slave traders, although in the beginning slaves who were already acclimatized were also shipped out of the islands. This overall region was relatively unimportant as a source of supply. There was a small increase in the number of slaves obtained there in the first few decades, but in general the trade did not prosper. They were not true Negroes, and their importation was often prohibited for religious motives, given Islamic influence among its inhabitants. They were known as Berber or Levantine slaves. In principle, the Spanish crown generally preferred Negroes from the more primitive parts of Africa, who could not contaminate the indigenous population of America with heretical ideas. However, the very fact that the prohibition had to be repeated so frequently is indicative that it was only partially obeyed. Royal decrees to this effect were promulgated in 1501, 1506, 1509, 1530, 1531, 1543, and 1550.[3] From the southern section of this region true Negroes were exported. These were known in Latin America as the Mandinga.

[1] Aguirre Beltrán, 1946; and Mellafe, 1959.

[2] A number of regional historians have dealt with this. For Argentina see Assadourian, 1965; and Scheuss de Studer, 1958. For Brazil see Goulart, 1949; and Boxer, 1969a. For Chile see Mellafe, 1959. For Colombia see Escalante, 1964. For Mexico see Aguirre Beltrán, 1946. For Peru see Lockhart, 1968. For Uruguay see Carvalho Neto, 1965. There is at least one general study: Curtin, 1969.

[3] Herrera, 1945; and Encinas, 1945. See also *Recopilación de Leyes de las Indias*, 1943. [The North Africans and Canary Islanders were basically Berbers, a Caucasian people. The Mauritanians were of mixed Negro and Berber stock. —Ed.]

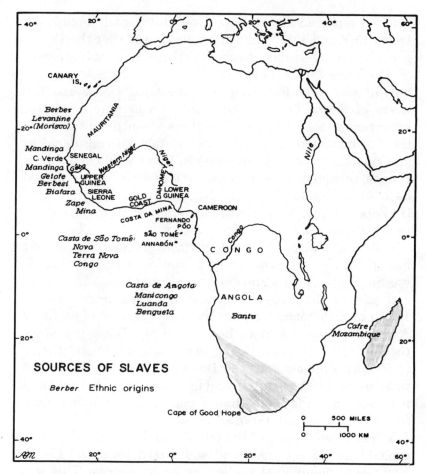

Map 4. Ethnic classifications of African slaves by region of origin.

2. The second region was of vast importance in the six-teenth century. It is the Upper Guinea or Cape Verde zone, lying between present-day Senegal and the Gêba River. It supplied a vast number of slaves for Portuguese, Dutch, and English traders in turn. These slaves were known in a vague, general way as slaves from the Guinea rivers, which in fact were none other than the western Niger River and its various ramifications. From here also came what was known in sixteenth century nomenclature as the Gelofe (or some-times Jelof), Berbesi, Biafara, and some of the Mandinga. The three great Portuguese trading posts in these areas

suffered repeated attacks from the Dutch and English between 1578 and 1585. The consequence was that the Portuguese began to rely more heavily on their slave trading center of São Tomé far to the south.

3. Immediately following was the Gold Coast and the rivers of Sierra Leone, which came to assume a relative importance toward the end of the sixteenth century. For the Portuguese these areas could in fact be considered as an extension of their possessions in Cape Verde and Upper Guinea, though now their interest was perhaps more centered on ivory and gold. The only Negroes embarked here were the Zape and the Mina, whom slave traders often used simply to declare as from Sierra Leone.[4]

4. At the end of the sixteenth century and in the first half of the seventeenth, the great center of the slave trade was São Tomé. This island dominated what is now Cameroon and part of the Congo. Negroes embarked there were of Bantu or Dahoman origin. In the local markets of all Latin America they were sold as the casta of São Tomé, the Novo, the Terra Nova, and the Congo, used as an ethnic designation (originally equivalent to the Bakongo). In 1599 São Tomé was captured by the Dutch, and in the century that followed it became nothing more than a convenient stopping place for slave ships of all nations.

5. The consequence of the fall of São Tomé was the rapid exploitation of the mainland southward from the Congo River and including the whole coast of Angola. This was the most important slave center from the middle of the seventeenth century onward. The slaves from here were usually known as the casta of Angola, although this term included other names, such as the Manicongo, the Luanda, and the Benguela.

6. The final zone is far more general than any of the above. It comprises the whole of the Portuguese seaborne empire east of the Cape of Good Hope: all the territories in East Africa, Asia, and the East Indies progressively occupied by

---

[4] Useful works on the history of the various regions in Africa where slaves were obtained, the characteristics of the trade in each locality, and the ethnic groups involved are Boxer, 1969a; Blake, 1937; Murdock, 1959; Curtin, 1969; and Herskovits, 1958.

Portugal after the voyage of Vasco da Gama in 1497-99. The Philippines are also to be included. The area widened and diversified to some degree the ethnic basis of the slaves brought to America. The East Africans were known as the Cafre or as the Mozambique, used often as loose ethnic terms. The word *chino*, Chinese, was used for anyone with Asian characteristics, though it is fairly certain that few or none were actually Chinese. Importation of slaves from Asia was occasional and relatively limited. In the first decades of the sixteenth century a number of Asian slaves arrived in the New World by way of Lisbon, along the normal routes. But the voyage of Miguel de Legazpi (1564-65) from the Pacific coast of Mexico to the Philippine Islands, established the more direct Manila-Acapulco route, which could be extended southward to link up with Panama, Guayaquil, and Callao. In this way a small but not inappreciable number of chino slaves came to Mexico and the other Spanish colonies on the Pacific seaboard, including Chile. Most of them were, however, Filipino rather than Chinese.[5]

Numbers of Slaves Imported

Transshipment and importation involved authorized ports of entry, which varied according to the times. These have been listed in Chapter 2. The most important on the basis of the number of piezas disembarked were undoubtedly Cartagena, Veracruz, Havana, Buenos Aires, Maranhão, Pernambuco, Salvador da Bahia, and Rio de Janeiro. There existed in all these ports and, in fact, in all the major towns, extensive barracoons which were used to house and store the slaves. These enclosures were the property of the asentistas or of the cabildos. Before any cargo of slaves could be unloaded and deposited in the barracoons, there were certain formalities. Local royal officials, a senior constable, and a representative of the governor or chief magistrate, as the case might be, came to check the legality of the shipment according to license, royal decree, or royal permit—papers

---

[5] Boxer, 1948; Schurz, 1959; and Chaunu, 1962. For further details about the chinos, see chap. 6.

for which the master of the vessel was responsible. Throughout the seventeenth century a health check was also required, under the medical supervision of a doctor, as a guard against smallpox or other infectious diseases, and quarantine was imposed on a ship when necessary.

When the system of ordinary licenses was superseded by asiento concessions, the above process became more complex. This was mainly owing to the replacement of the per capita basis of the licenses by the notion of pieza in the asientos. It was necessary to determine the relative equivalence of the slaves in the cargo in terms of piezas, so as to calculate the appropriate import duty. Two phases were involved. The first, known technically as the *palmeo*, constituted measuring each slave in turn. To be considered a full pieza a slave had to be more than 7 palms, or 5 feet, 7 inches (1.70 meters) tall. A physical examination and some calculation as to age were also included. The second phase was termed the *carimba*, both the word and the process being Portuguese in origin. The carimba was a small mark branded on some part of the body; the back, chest, or thigh. The mark varied according to the asentista and the port of entry. It was intended to be a guarantee to prospective purchasers that the slave had entered legally and that appropiate duties had been paid.[6]

It has already been stated that a further concept developed at the end of the seventeenth century when Domingo Grillo obtained his concessions, and especially when the Portuguese recouped some part of the trade through the Royal Guinea Company. This was the idea of the *tonelada* or tonnage of African slaves.[7] A greater complication of the importation processes was the result. By that time, the consulados in the colonies had acquired the right to collect some of the taxes associated with the import and sale of slaves. What is more, they had the right to collect a further tax on the export of the precious metals which had been paid for the slaves. The consulados often farmed out or sold off their

[6] Further information about the process can be had from Martin, 1931; Mellafe, 1959; Scheuss de Studer, 1958; and Goulart, 1949. See also Biblioteca Municipal de Lima, Cedulario del Cabildo, vols. III and XXVI; and Archivo Nacional de Lima, Sección Histórica, Esclavos, Legajo 1. For pieza de Indias, see chap. 2, n. 21.

[7] See chap. 2, n. 22.

collection rights. The consequence was an endless series of lawsuits, legal difficulties, and economic problems. The slaving companies paid the Spanish crown under their asiento agreements dues based on tonnage, whereas local import duties and sales taxes were still based on the *per capita* system. An example of the litigation is the case between the representatives of the Royal Guinea Company in Lima on the one hand and the fiscal authorities and consulado of the city on the other. Through the long proceedings of the case, it became clear that when negotiations were originally undertaken between the asentistas and the crown, the criterion of the crown had been that one ton of slaves was equivalent to one slave who could be considered a complete pieza. It was only afterwards that the crown had accepted an equivalence of three slaves to a ton. It also became manifest that in practice it was generally and tacitly accepted that up to seven slaves could be included in a ton.[8]

Shipping was important in a number of other ways. In the sixteenth century it was forbidden to ship any other merchandise in the slavers, but pressures brought about by European powers entering into the field caused the crown to make concessions. Spain's growing economic crisis and the consequent acute shortage of shipping likewise led to significant changes. Henceforth the companies themselves had to provide vessels. In the sixteenth century, it was specifically stipulated that the ship was not to be an *urca* (traditionally purely a freight vessel), since it was slow and clumsy and therefore easy prey to buccaneers. But the slave companies went further and developed special boats for the trade. They devised security systems designed to prevent escapes and mutinies. Below deck, cargo space was developed to the maximum so as to fit in as many slaves as possible. The average tonnage of slavers up to the mid-seventeenth century was 118 tons. From then on it rose to the order of 220 tons, some vessels even reaching 500 tons.[9] The average tonnage of slave ships and the frequency of arrival in Ameri-

[8] Archivo Nacional de Lima, Sección Histórica, Esclavos, Legajo 1. Not taking this type of document into account has been the basis of some notable errors in estimating the number of slaves imported in Latin America.

[9] Chaunu, 1956-59, vol. VI; and G. Martin, 1931. Ships' tonnage expressed here is the toneladas mentioned before (chap. 2, n. 22).

can ports provide a valuable means to calculate, although only approximately and tentatively, the number of Africans imported through these ports. It is obvious that this estimate can only apply to legally imported slaves, since it is impossible to discover the numbers brought to America as contraband. Over the 89 years from 1551 to 1640, 1,223 slave vessels legally docked in Spanish America. This is equivalent to 144,314 tons, which in turn implies that approximately 350,-000 Africans of both sexes and all ages were legally imported in just this period alone. As far as is known, licenses and monopolistic concessions granted by the crown in the same period were for only approximately 100,000 slaves.[10]

It has not been possible to know precisely how many slaves came to the New World. Smuggling is one facet of the problem, but there was also the question of underregistration of slave ships, and in the case of the Spanish colonies, the circumstances of the annuities, which have already been described. An alternative method of calculation for the Spanish colonies has been attempted. It is equally risky and tentative, but at least if provides a further line of reference. It is the income derived by the royal treasury as a result of the issuance of licenses, or annuities converted into licenses. Although the structure of the Spanish treasury is fairly well known, the process can only be approximate, since the accounts themselves are not overclear, particularly for the annuities. There was not necessarily a direct relationship between the annual income received by the treasury as a result of the slave trade and the number of slaves actually imported in any one year. The latter ultimately depended on the availability and accumulation of slaves for export in Africa, and also on the availability and capacity of the shipping operated by the asentistas or by holders of import licenses. During the entire colonial period the tendency of the Spanish crown was to sell many more licenses than could ever be used, in fact many more than were appropriate to its own slave policy. This surplus of licenses was manifestly the consequence of the treasury's severe financial straits. For

---

[10] These details have been obtained mainly from the works mention in nn. 2 and 6 in this chapter; and also from H. and P. Chaunu, 1956-59, vols. VI and VIII.

example, in a year when only 3,000 slaves were to be imported, the actual amount collected could well be for twice as many in terms of licenses. Even this latter figure is likely to be less than the total number of other licenses issued in previous years but not due to come into effect until the year in question. Despite the complexities and uncertainties outlined, figures obtained in this way are very similar to those based on calculations using the tonnage of the vessels in the trade. Between 1551 and 1640, the royal treasury seems to have received amounts corresponding to the importation of 337,200 *piezas*. Extending this period backward to 1511 gives a total figure of 371,400 piezas.[11]

It has already been indicated that there is inadequate knowledge of all the licenses and contracts signed between the crown and the slave traders and companies, so that it is highly risky to venture an opinion of how many slaves the king actually allowed to be taken to the colonies. However, it is not totally irrelevant to include what facts there are. Up to the year 1773, including the concession given to the General Company of Negroes of Aguirre and Arístegui[12] but excluding the whole final phase of free commerce, it is possible to calculate on the basis of official documents a figure of 516,114 imported Africans. If one applies the gap noted above between royal concessions and the average calculated by vessel tonnage, it is possible to come to a figure of not less than 1,500,000. It is worth emphasizing that this does not take into account such factors as free trade, the increase in ship tonnage, the smaller concessions (mentioned in previous chapters) given as outright grants by the monarch, and finally but most importantly, the virtually uncontrolled smuggling of more than two centuries. Perhaps one could hazard an opinion that approxiamtely three million slaves were imported into Spanish America in the colonial period.

It is difficult to assess what all the above figures mean in terms of comparative volume of trade. In the years just after 1560, following on a rise in the price of licenses, the Spanish crown derived an annual average of 136,030 silver

---

[11] Carande, 1949; and Ulloa, 1963, have been extremely useful works in making these calculations.
[12] See p. 60.

pesos from the sale of importation rights for slaves.[13] In 1561 the wholesale value of all the slaves imported was equivalent to 22.5 percent of the entire silver production of the Viceroyalty of Peru, and this happened to be a year of particularly high production, especially for the mines of Potosí.[14] In 1589 the Casa de la Contratación, in a report to the king, made mention of the exportation of slaves to America as being "the most important item of merchandise" taken to the Indies. In 1594, for example, 47.9 percent of the vessels arriving in Spanish America were slave ships.[15]

Despite the fact that the slave trade became progressively more independent of the general commerce and economic tendencies of the Spanish empire, it still suffered, at least until the middle of the seventeenth century, from the fluctuations endemic to all of Spain's merchant trade. Pierre Chaunu has shown clearly the relationship between general economic recessions and the crises of the slave trade in the years of 1603-1605 and 1611-1616. In this sense the slave trade with the Spanish possessions differed somewhat from Portuguese trade with America. The latter grew steadily, whereas the Spanish slave trade underwent a lengthy critical period of ups and downs.[16]

The case of Brazil is similar to Spanish America in terms of the total numbers of slaves imported, but dissimilar in the way this number was distributed over almost the four centuries that the trade lasted there. One specialist has calculated that in the century from 1570 to 1670, 400,000 slaves were introduced into Brazil, this being before its economic boom. From the beginning of the eighteenth century, the Portuguese colonies became one of the major markets in the New World. Between 1811 and 1870, Brazil received

---

[13] The royal treasury used ducats for its accounts. The sum quoted in the text was approximately equivalent to 100,000 ducats (Ulloa, 1963). A ducat was worth 370 maravedíes, whereas a silver peso (*peso de plata corriente*) was worth 272 maravedíes. A peso of fine gold was worth 450 maravedíes; it was largely a unit of measure for bookkeeping at this time.

[14] The year 1561 has been taken for the purposes of this calculation because the production of silver was so high: 783,234,088 maravedíes (Jara, 1966). On the other hand, the value of the slaves imported has been kept at a deliberately conservative estimate: 2600 slaves at a price of 250 silver pesos each would give a total sum of 176,800,000 maravedíes.

[15] Mellafe, 1959.

[16] H. and P. Chaunu, 1956-59, vol. VI; and Mauro, 1956.

60.3 percent of all the slaves disembarked in Latin America. 3,646,800 African slaves were imported into Brazil.[17]

Ports of Entry and Legal and Illegal Routes

Apart from contraband slaves, the initial phase of importation ended with the arrival of shipments of slaves in officially designated ports. In practice, up to 1605 with the asiento granted to Gonzalo Vaz, an asentista, or his representatives was unable to go beyond these ports to sell his slaves in the local markets of Spanish America. The prohibition was gradually relaxed until, at the end of the seventeenth century, slave importers were allowed freedom of movement on both sea and land. In spite of this, many companies preferred to sell their slaves on a wholesale basis or to carry on their trade along the coastline rather than run the risk of possible losses through mortality on long overland journeys, costs of feeding, and other hazards. On the other hand, they renounced the opportunity for the higher prices they could have obtained by retailing their slaves in the interior. Brazil aside, the only exceptions to this preference for coastal trade were the central interior regions of Mexico and Peru, because of their high silver production. Slave importers were sometimes able to obtain limited permission to go into central Mexico for the purposes of trade, but they were never able to do so in Peru. They had to use Spaniards and local people of Spanish descent, the Creoles, in order to circumvent the various customs barriers and restrictions.

The distribution of African slaves in Spanish America was therefore normally undertaken by a second group of traders, slave traders on a smaller scale—Europeans or Creoles who also traded in local products and who imported goods from Spain. Their activities were organized so as to follow certain land and sea routes, which in combination formed a characteristic pattern throughout the colonial period. There were four main geographical areas of emphasis, at least insofar as slaves imported legally across the Atlantic were concerned (see map 5). The first was the Caribbean island region. It was not dominated by any single authorized port of entry

[17] Mauro, 1956; Curtin, 1969; and Goulart, 1949.

but rather by several, the most important being Havana, Santo Domingo, and San Juan. The Spanish crown almost throughout the whole colonial period granted them fixed quotas, and here the question of internal distribution was minimal. The second area was the mainland of Mexico and part of Central America, which were for a long time supplied through Veracruz. At the end of the seventeenth century, several ports on the Bay of Campeche and the coast of Honduras were also included as authorized ports.

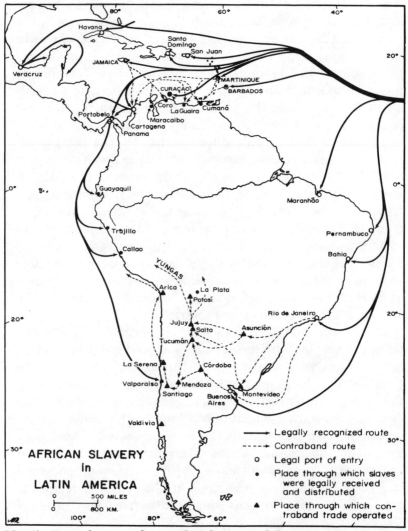

Map 5. Ports of entry and internal trade routes of the major colonial powers in Latin America to 1789.

The third region was perhaps the most important in the quantities of slaves received and distributed. It had as its center the port of Cartagena. Some part of its cargoes of slaves passed on to the Pacific across Panama. Some of the slaves remained in Central America, but others were distributed along the Venezuelan coast and in the interior of the Province of Santa Fe de Bogotá by means of the Magdalena River. In the sixteenth century, slaves began to be imported through other points along the Venezuelan coast: Maracaibo, Coro, La Guaira, and Cumaná. This of course tended to limit somewhat the prominence of Cartagena as the major port.[18] The Spanish authorities from time to time allowed limited cargoes to be disembarked in these smaller ports, and in others in Yucatán and on the Atlantic coast of Central America, as part of an effort to check clandestine trade in slaves. The English, French, and Dutch, on the other hand, established small trading posts in inlets and bays. Frequently they entered into pacts with the chieftains of isolated tribes, who were useful as points of contact and as sources of labor in their commercial activities. Spanish and Creole smugglers, acting as middlemen for landowners and mine owners in the interior, would come to these places to obtain their supplies of slaves. Official attempts to regain control of the coasts were never very successful. Military incursions against mestizo and Indian groups who supported the smuggling, especially the Goajiros, likewise availed the Spaniards very little.[19]

The fourth zone was the basin of the Plata, served by Buenos Aires. However, this port, together with Paraguay and other provinces, became important in overland routes developed by contraband rather than by official trade within a policy of careful control of trade. This subject will be considered later. The Andean provinces along the Pacific seaboard, on the other hand, relied for more than two centuries on Panama as the only legal port of entry, the

---

[18] The above refers only to trading in African slaves. For general commerce between the various regions, there were other extremely important local routes; for example, between Venezuela and Mexico. See Arcila Farías, 1950; and Ramos, 1970.

[19] Interesting documents concerning these attempts at control may be consulted in the Archivo Nacional de Colombia, Sección Colonial, Caciques e Indios, vols. 4, 33, and 47. The Goajiros are the Indian inhabitants of the peninsula of Goajira, the northernmost tip of Colombia (see map 3).

slaves coming through Cartagena and Portobelo. Panama at the time was obviously vital in connecting the Pacific provinces of South America with Europe. Also, it came to be a key port in what could be known as the Pacific Ocean route, that is, the route connecting Valdivia in the south of Chile, Valparaíso, Callao, Guayaquil, Panama, Acapulco, and the Philippines. This is not to say, however, that more direct routes were not used between the Far East and Panama or Callao.[20] The Pacific route, then, was involved with both African slaves by way of the Atlantic and with a much smaller number of so-called Chinese slaves embarked in the Philippines. Spain considered the Panama route to be absolutely essential to its economic wellbeing, and maintained it with whatever power it could, a policy wholeheartedly supported by the Consulados of Seville and Lima. The opposite was the case with the provinces of Charcas, Paraguay, Tucumán, Cuyo, Córdoba, Buenos Aires, and even Chile. The merchants and producers of these areas could find no outlet for their products, nor could they maintain any significant level of imports in European manufactured goods or slaves without the removal of restrictions and the opening up of commerce through Buenos Aires.[21] The inland provinces of Peru and the regions of Upper Peru and Chile tended to resent the Panama-Callao route, since their own development depended utterly upon it, but by the end of the sixteenth century the route was incapable of accommodating their natural economic growth; what is more, it was overburdened with customs requirements, tariffs, and taxes which had severe inhibiting effects.[22]

The insistence of Spanish official policy on keeping the slave trade within certain established routes had two main motives: to prevent the outflow of precious metals and the inflow of contraband slaves. The latter implied not only gold and silver in payment for them, but also tax evasion and official corruption. All these thrived, despite Spain's efforts to the contrary, right up to the inception of free trade.

[20] Schurz, 1959; Borah, 1954; Moreyra Paz-Soldán, 1944; and Mellaffe, 1959.

[21] Céspedes del Castillo, 1947; Levene, 1952; Rodríguez, 1956; Kossok, 1959; Assadourian, 1965; and Zuluaga, 1970.

[22] Céspedes del Castillo, 1947; Levene, 1952; Rodríguez, 1956; Assadourian, 1965; and Mellafe, 1959.

Clandestine trade became so common as to appear almost the norm throughout the colonial period. It was a trade that operated along the Atlantic coasts, since to move slaves into the Pacific and to trade from there was too expensive and risky to make it worthwhile. The first great center for smuggling was the Caribbean. The plantation economy which developed there apace throughout the seventeenth century badly needed abundant, cheap labor. The native population which had survived from the previous century lived in wilder regions outside the zones of European settlement. Besides, the foreign powers involved in the slave trade maintained such storage centers as Jamaica, Curaçao, and Barbados near at hand, where slaves could be easily exchanged for sugar, cacao, tobacco, pearls, and other goods.

In the South Atlantic region of Spanish America, it was not the needs of a plantation economy which supported slave contraband so much as it was mining in the Andes and stock raising in the basin of La Plata. Because of the needs of the Andean and Plata regions, there developed an extensive overland commercial route, which in a sense was the diametric opposite of the Panama-Callao sea route. The continental route ran from the South Atlantic seaboard into the interior, up and even over the Andes to the Pacific coast. It was a complex route with numerous ramifications, all related to commerce in slaves. The first significant contraband carried along this route had its point of departure in Paraguay, using slaves obtained from Portuguese and Creole merchants in Brazil. The route divided at Salta, the more important branch going northward through Jujuy to Upper Peru, and particularly to the silver mines of Potosí. The other branch went southwards through Tucumán and Mendoza, and finally to Chile. However, what perhaps came to be the classic continental route was organized at the beginning of the seventeenth century with its point of departure in Buenos Aires. It again had two main branches, the more important and profitable one northwards through Córdoba, Tucumán, Salta, and Jujuy to its destination in the city of La Plata (Upper Peru, the present-day Sucre) and Potosí. It provided African labor for the industries and commercial enterprises of Upper Peru and the more interior, wilder regions known as the provinces of the Andes and Yungas. The other branch consisted of a deviation southwestwards at Córdoba down to Mendoza, and to Santiago in Chile. It extended up the coast through Valparaíso to Coquimbo and La Serena to Arica and to a number of small ports north of Arica. It thus supplied slaves to the warm and fertile coastal valleys of Peru.[23] In the seventeenth century, although trade in Africans never really ceased along the legal Pacific route, it went into almost total decline, whereas the overland clandestine trade became more and more important.[24] The measures taken by the crown, the Peruvian viceroys, and the royal officials of all these provinces to prevent or control such trade achieved little. The establishment of a customs station in Córdoba (the Aduana Seca de Córdoba) in 1662 had perhaps some effect, but in fact it simply meant that the trade avoided Córdoba altogether and detoured through other places. The transfer of the customs station of Jujuy in 1695 accomplished as little.

The Marketing of Slaves

The fact that some of the Spanish provinces were served by recognized, direct ports of entry for slaves, whereas others had to rely legally on more indirect trade carried out along extensive routes was important in various ways. The shortage of slaves in such places as the province of Quito, the viceroyalty of Peru and Chile, together with the higher prices obtainable for them, made the more indirect trade extremely lucrative. On the other hand, it demanded large capital for such things as purchase and maintenance of slaves, payments of taxes and tariffs, cost of transport over long distances, the frequent necessity to treat illnesses, the provision of clothing, and even the fattening of slaves so as to gain better prices in the local markets. One of the fundamental differences between slave traders involved in this trade is that

[23] On these routes see the works indicated in the two previous notes, and also Jaimes Freire 1915; and Levillier, 1915 and 1920 (see Section 2 of Bibliography); and Canabrava, 1944; and Torre Revello, 1958.

[24] Mellafe, 1959. For documents see Biblioteca Nacional de Lima, Sección Manuscritos, C456 and D177; Archivo Nacional de Lima, Tribunal del Consulado, Legajo 10, Cuaderno 137; and Archivo Nacional de Santiago, Colección Real Audiencia, vols. 45, 88, 131, 187, and 316.

the former were mainly interested in the total volume of their cargoes. They were not interested in the fairly high mortality and level of illness, which they wrote off as a normal loss. The slave traders within Spanish America, on the other hand, purchased much smaller numbers, between five and one hundred Negroes, and they took whatever measures they could to safeguard their capital investment, which frequently resulted in a more humane treatment of their slaves.

The large capital sums required for such trade were normally raised, from the time of the conquest onward, by local associations of merchants, who had interests in many ventures besides that of slave trading.[25] These associations existed in all the larger towns and ports, where the capital resources of the individual provinces were concentrated. This concentration, together with the marked centralization of political, administrative, and commercial life, meant that the slaves were marketed in large urban centers, such as Mexico City, Veracruz, Bahia, Lima, and Santiago, rather than at the particular points of production where the labor was needed. Entrepreneurs and producers had to go to these centers to purchase their slaves, or commission other, more modest merchants to this end—merchants who traveled to the most remote corners of the provinces.

Prices charged for slaves varied enormously from place to place on the continent in relation to the distances involved, the difficulties encountered, and shortage of transportation facilities. The crown was never able to impose an effective price control system, though it attempted to do so on various occasions. Slave prices were obviously determined partly by the slaves themselves—their condition, type, and so on—and partly by the condition of the market, the state of the economy, and even the policies of Spain and Portugal in relation to the colonies and to the other European powers interested in slavery. There were four major factors to which prices were generally subject.

1. In the sixteenth century, prices of imported goods were inflated by the fact that a new economy was then being

---

[25] Mellafe, 1959; Assadourian, 1965; and Zuluaga, 1970.

developed in the New World, the fundamental characteristic of which was the exchange of relatively abundant gold for scarce European commodities. Inflated import prices were especially true of the initial years of European occupation of each region. A graph plotted over the first few decades in regard to slave prices, or prices of other imported goods, would show an appreciable drop in each area, whereas the general tendency of world prices at the time was to the contrary. The drop in the American region occurred in strict relation to the degree of success that the Europeans had had in establishing themselves in each area, and to the extent to which trade between the various areas had developed.

2. One of the major factors involved in differentiation of slave prices between one place and another was the varying distance from the appropriate port of entry. Prices were in general high everywhere in the first years of occupation, but they were far higher in the more remote provinces. For example, in Mexico City the average price for an ordinary slave dropped from 200 gold pesos in 1525 to a little over 100 around the period 1538-40. There was a similar drop in prices in Lima, but within a much wider range. The average in 1536 was 360 gold pesos, and in 1548, 140 pesos. In Santiago, Chile, the average price in the 1540s was 300 gold pesos, twice as high as in Lima, three times as high as in Mexico, and almost five times as high as in the Caribbean. By about 1615 the price in Santiago had dropped relatively little, to 265 pesos.[26]

3. Special taxes, duties, and tariffs had a fundamental effect on the price to the purchaser, especially in the seventeenth and eighteenth centuries. These charges were particularly large for the provinces that had to rely on the Panama-Callao route. Around 1630 the average price for an African slave shipped down the Pacific route was 500 silver pesos

[26] The prices quoted here and in the following paragraphs have been taken from Saco, 1937-44; Díaz-Soler, 1953; Aguirre Beltrán, 1946; Acosta Saignes, 1961a; Scheuss de Studer, 1958; Assadourian, 1965 and 1966; Zuluaga, 1970; Lockhart, 1968; and Mellafe, 1959. Relevant published documents can be found in Lohmann Villena, 1941-44; Millares Carlo and Mantecón, 1945-46; and Friede, 1955-57. Very useful have been unpublished documents taken from the records of notaries public of the National Archives of Lima and Santiago. See also Archivo General de Indias, Lima, Legajo 1095.

in Lima, 800 in Potosí, and 600 in Santiago. On the other hand, in the same year, slaves brought by the overland contraband route from Buenos Aires would cost the colonial traders about 150 silver pesos, but would be sold for more than 200. Such differences in cost were bound to assure the success of the overland route and the increase of contraband.

Additional, imposed costs, which ultimately had to be paid by the consumer, were common to the Portuguese colonies also. Agricultural producers in Brazil complained in 1612 that the excessive taxes which they had to pay for Africans in Angola prevented them from importing labor essential to increase production.[27] Planters in the Peruvian coastal valleys a century later tried on many occasions to have abolished a tax based on the resale of slaves subsequent to the initial purchase, but they had no success. They claimed that it was common for a slave to change hands twenty to thirty times in his life, and that the total sum paid in these taxes amounted to more than the price paid for his initial purchase.[28]

4. Finally, there was a general tendency, especially from the middle of the seventeenth century onward, for a continuous increase in slave prices. This followed the general pattern of world prices and monetary devaluation of the times. However, prices for slaves were frequently affected by a sudden demand for labor, vast new opportunities in mining, greater need for agricultural goods, and interruptions suffered by trade as a result of war. For example, the prices for Africans in Lima at the end of the seventeenth century were never less than 600 silver pesos. In Buenos Aires, which imported slaves directly, prices rose from 240 pesos in 1774 to 300 in 1802. Around the same time in Cuba, the price did not drop below 300 silver pesos. Brazil was an area which experienced sudden increases in demand for slaves with the booms in mining in Minas Gerais and Goiás in the first half of the eighteenth century, and in coffee zones, such as Vassouras, in the nineteenth. Slave prices suffered rises similar to those in Spanish America. Also, around the middle

[27] Sluiter, 1949.
[28] Archivo General de Indias, Lima, Legajo 1095, no. 99.

of the nineteenth century, Britain's abolitionist policies, as carried out by its diplomacy and its navy, made even more acute the shortage of slaves, especially in such places as Brazil, Cuba, and Puerto Rico.[29]

The quality of the slaves themselves was obviously important in determining prices; youth, strength, health, and the ability to perform some manual trade or specialized work was prized. The technical language of the period made various significant distinctions. A child up to seven was called a *mulequillo*; up to twelve, *muleque*; and up to sixteen, *mulecón*. Prices were, naturally, proportionate to age. The new arrivals were known as *bozales*, a term that implied that they were as yet unfamiliar with Castilian, and that their good and bad qualities and their capacity for work were unknown. The word *bozal* would then appear in the documents of sale drawn up before a notary public, to ensure the vendor's immunity against claims of responsibility if the slave happened to turn out badly or become sick later on. There were two expressions that meant the opposite of bozal. One was *ladino*, used for Negroes who had been born in Africa but who had adopted the language and customs of Spanish America. The second term was *criollo*, or Creole, used in this context specifically for those of African blood but born in America. These circumstances in themselves did not really alter the price, but they were involved with custom and law which obliged the vendor to state the defects and illnesses which such slaves had. These defects are found in a number of frequently repeated formulas in the bills of sale: "I am selling him because he is a thief," "because he drinks too much" or "tries to escape" or "because he is a cimarrón," and so on. The defect that brought the price down most was that of cimarrón, since it generally meant that he had been punished by the law as a runaway or fugitive slave, or for some serious crime.[30]

[29] Boxer, 1969a; Stein, 1970; and Díaz Soler, 1953. Britain outlawed the British slave trade in 1807, and abolished slavery in the British West Indies in 1833. For further details on Britain's role in abolition in Latin America, see chap. 6 below.

[30] Further details are given in Mellafe, 1959.

PLATES

Plate 1 Living quarters of a slave ship, mid-nineteenth century.
(Maurice Rugendas, 1853)

Plate 2 Unloading slaves at Rio de Janeiro in the nineteenth century.
(Maurice Rugendas, 1853)

Plate 3 Public slave market in Brazil, early nineteenth century.
(Maurice Rugendas, 1853)

Plate 4 Sale of a contraband slave in the Antilles, early nineteenth century.
(Captain Canot, 1854)

5 Branding a female contraband slave in the Antilles,
early nineteenth century. (Captain Canot, 1854)

facing page:

6 Slave farm worker in northern Peru, latter part of the
eighteenth century. (Trujillo del Peru, 1936)

7 Female slave farm worker in the north of Peru,
late eighteenth century. (Trujillo del Peru, 1936)

Plate 7

Plate 6

facing page:

9 Black slaves working in a refining mill in northern Peru, eighteenth century. (Trujillo del Peru, 1936)

10 A wealthy woman of mixed African and Indian blood (zamba) in the Viceroyalty of Peru, late eighteenth century. (Trujillo del Peru, 1936)

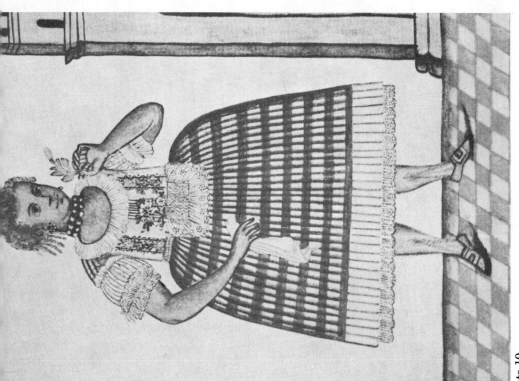

Plate 10

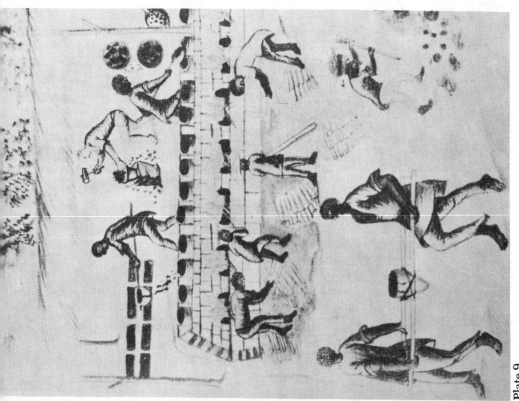

Plate 9

12 Musical entertainment of blacks and black mestizos in Peru, late eighteenth century. (Trujillo del Peru, 1936)

11 African slave music and dancing in Trujillo, Peru, eighteenth century. (Trujillo del Peru, 1936)

13 Mistreatment of slaves by their Spanish masters in Peru, early seventeenth century. (Felipe Guaman Poma de Ayala, 1936)

14 Public whipping of slaves in Brazil, mid-nineteenth century. (Maurice Rugendas, 1853)

CHAPTER FOUR

COLONIAL ECONOMIC STRUCTURE AND NEGRO SLAVERY

Mining and Slavery

Gold and silver, obtained as booty or through mining operations played a vital role in financing the conquest and consolidation of the Spanish empire. From the sixteenth century onward, the economy of the empire was deeply involved in the production of precious metals, which reached a peak in the early seventeenth century and then declined. Production revived in the last decades of the eighteenth century. On the other hand, in Brazil it was the tardy discovery of gold in comparison with that in the Spanish colonies which gave the metal an importance it had not previously had.

Labor scarcity was a chronic problem in most New World silver and gold mining regions. Although solutions to this difficulty varied considerably from one epoch to another, African slavery always played some role in alleviating labor shortages. In the sixteenth century the high rate of return to miners and the existence of widespread gold deposits acted as a strong incentive for the importation of slaves to all of the newly established colonies. African slaves were utilized for gold mining everywhere, although the supply of slaves was uncertain and they were particularly expensive. In Peru, for example, after the conquest slaves were used, intermingled with groups of native workers, to wash the precious metal. The local Indian population helped with supplementary tasks and with the providing of food. Chile resembled Peru in having a large native population and being a remote area where slaves were incredibly expensive. Here, too, at Curahoma and Valdivia, they worked for gold with the Indians. The output of the African slave and the profitability of his production were such that one year of work usually covered his original purchase price.[1]

Over the second half of the sixteenth century such placer mines disappeared rapidly. But silver, more abundant though offering a smaller return per worker, was developing in importance with the mines of Porco and Potosí in Upper Peru, and Zacatecas and San Luis Potosí in Mexico.[2] After the conquest, the conquistadors, with their sense for business opportunities, initially assumed responsibility for these great mines. They attempted to repeat there the success they had had with slaves elsewhere, but they failed. The mine of Porco, for example, clearly showed that silver worked by Negro slaves *en masse* was not economic, save in exceptional cases. In 1554 and 1555 the Council of Indies took a hand in the matter and made its views quite clear. Following the opinions of experienced silver miners, the Council decided that the best method for deep shaft mining would be to use Indian labor on a moderate scale, with appropriate payment for their work. In 1570, Viceroy Francisco de Toledo implemented this policy in Peru. He regrouped the dispersed and diminished Indian population into large villages, and also established compulsory service in the mines, the *mita minera*.[3]

The consequence, then, was that Africans were never used on a large scale in mining after the shift away from gold

[1] Ortíz de Zúñiga, 1920-25; and Mellafe, 1959.

[2] Mellafe, 1959; and Wolf, 1964. Also Archivo Nacional de Santiago, Colección Gay-Morla, vol. 120. For Mexico, see, for example, Berthe, 1958. (Also see chap. 2, n. 2, above, on Charles V.) By 1540 silver formed 85 percent of the official shipment of precious metals from the New World to Spain by weight, and 40 percent by value. By the 1560s silver had come to exceed gold in value as well. See J. H. Parry, *The Spanish Seaborne Empire* (London, 1966, pp. 105 ff.).

[3] Levillier, 1929; and Villarán, 1964. The mita system extended to other services considered to be in the public interest besides mining. It was a levy of forced labor from Indian communities in which workers were selected by lots. The length of service, at fixed wage rates, depended on the task to which the *mitayos* were assigned (mining was usually for 10 months). Official legislation was quite precise in these respects and others (e.g., distances of place of work from the communities, the avoidance of changes of climatic conditions, persons to be excluded), although in practice the system was clearly open to abuse.

to silver production. They were, nonetheless, never totally divorced from it, given their capacity for work and also the favorable experience the Spaniards had had with them as auxiliaries in the conquest. They were placed in charge of groups of other workers; they were used as watchmen. In some places such slaves received the name of *sayapayos* and were subject to legislation regulating their activities and functions.[4] Slaves also formed an important segment of the labor force in the refining mills where ores were crushed and the precious metals removed. To perform these services slaves were still in demand, for example, in Potosí, especially when the production of silver began to fall alarmingly at the beginning of the seventeenth century. In 1608 the royal officials of Potosí wrote to the king, saying that, despite the fact that experience had shown it to be uneconomic to work the silver mines with Negro slaves, it would be desirable to allow 1500 or 2000 slaves a year to be brought up the Rio de la Plata in order to perform tasks which were drawing Indian labor away from work in the mine shafts.[5] Such petitions were repeated with more and more urgency and arguments, but with little success. In fact, it was even suggested that the whole native labor force be gradually replaced by slaves, in spite of the experience of the past and the advice of specialists at the time.[6]

Another factor which continued to associate a fairly high percentage of Negro slaves with mining in Latin America was the almost complete lack of an Indian or mestizo population in many areas where important finds were made. Such finds could only be successful with a high per capita yield. One must cite the high concentration of Negroes in such areas in Brazil from the beginning of the eighteenth century, and also in the copper mines of Cuba and the gold mining regions on the Pacific coast of Colombia and Ecuador.[7] Another good example is the copper mines of Cocorote in Venezuela in the seventeenth century, operated by the royal

---

[4] Medina, 1889-95, vol. 29; and Mellafe, 1959.
[5] Archivo General de Indias, Audiencia de Charcas, 35.
[6] Archivo General de Indias, Audiencia de Charcas, 32; and Leon Pinelo, 1623 and 1624 (for Leon Pinelo, see Section 2 of Bibliography).
[7] Cevallos, 1886-89, vol. IV.

treasury and combined with a dockyard worked by slaves.[8] Many regions constantly petitioned for slaves on the grounds that it was impossible to get other labor to develop new discoveries, imaginary or real.[9] Throughout the second half of the seventeenth and all of the eighteenth century, mining districts, such as Copiapó in Chile and Parral in Mexico, came to rely more and more on paid labor, so that the ethnic and racial distinctions became blurred among the miners. The black population, slave and free, together with a high percentage of black mixed-bloods, formed an important part of this new social group of workers.[10]

Agriculture and Slavery

In discussing agriculture, there is an obvious distinction to be drawn between production associated with local requirements and tropical crop production designed for export. Both involved slavery. The need to feed a local population and provide for internal trade within the continent required slaves for a number of reasons. First, large urban centers and major communication lines were the first to suffer a critical shortage in Indian workers. These had to be supplemented or replaced by Africans. It is not a coincidence that local authorities in many places explained the various crises in food supply by the lack of slave labor for agriculture. It is hardly surprising, in this context, that such cities as Lima, Mexico City, and Rio de Janeiro came to have major concentrations of Negroes.[11]

Second, there was the tendency to use a large part of the Indian population for mining or manufacturing, to the point that whatever time they had for their rudimentary agriculture could hardly have contributed to an increase in food production and the creation of a surplus. Food shortages reached a critical point in some of the provinces in the eighteenth century. In Peru there was serious antagonism,

[8] Acosta Saignes, 1956; see map 3.
[9] Anuncibay, 1963; and Jaramillo Uribe, 1963.
[10] West, 1949; E. Wolf, 1953; and Carmagnani, 1963.
[11] For Lima, Moreyra Paz-Soldán and Céspedes del Castillo, 1954-55, vol. III: Biblioteca Municipal de Lima, Cedulario del Cabildo, Tomos VIII and IX; and Lockhart, 1968.

economically and socially, between those who employed what labor there was in mining and those who wanted to use it for agriculture.[12] A useful supply of labor could well have been created, at the end of the sixteenth century, by crown policies which aimed at protecting native communities through prohibiting the use of Indians in manufacturing, sugar mills, and tropical cultivation. However, these policies were not put into effect and consequently did nothing to relieve the demand for African agricultural workers.[13] On the other hand, the important urban centers in the Portuguese colonies, Salvador da Bahia, Rio de Janeiro, São Paulo, were simply not in a position to entertain any possibility of using Indian, mestizo, or European labor to supply local markets with agricultural produce.[14]

The high profits from growing agricultural commodities for domestic consumption was an important factor in drawing slave labor into this sector of the colonial economy. Before debt peonage became widespread, farmers who specialized in supplying food stuffs to large urban centers had difficulty in retaining enough Indian or mestizo labor. There is considerable documentation that attests to the profitability of using slaves for this work. The priest Ovalle, discussing central Chile in the middle of the seventeenth century, puts it this way: "So high are the profits to be made (from the sale of agricultural products) that there must be many people who, on a basis of 40,000 pesos or less invested in land, livestock, and the slaves to care for both, must earn 10,000 to 12,000 pesos, which is a profit rate of 25 percent, and too high a one not to be a matter of conscience."[15] An active agricultural commerce was established between the fertile lowlands and valleys of the Andean region and the densely populated mining centers in Bolivia and in some of the mountain provinces of Peru. This farming relied on the labor of Negroes in increasing numbers. Its main products were wine and spirits. In 1615 in the coastal Peruvian valleys of

[12] Mellafe, 1965b.
[13] Villarán, 1964; and Gibson, 1964.
[14] Westin de Cerqueira, 1967.
[15] Ovalle, 1888, vol. I. Alonso de Ovalle (1601-1651) was a Jesuit priest born in Santiago. His *Histórica relación* (published first in Rome in 1646) has the merit of being the first general history of Chile.

Ica and Pisco alone, 20,000 Negroes worked in the vineyards.[16] The sugar-producing valleys of the northern Peruvian coast also utilized, for the same reasons, large numbers of slaves. The valley of Moche, where the city of Trujillo is situated, had 3650 Negroes and mulattoes working in plantations and mills in the period round 1760. As many were in the nearby valleys of Virú and Chicama.[17]

In the agricultural sector the demand for African slaves was highest on tropical plantations. Here slaves were used on a massive scale, and increasingly so up to the end of the colonial period. The plantation areas were the northern coasts of South America, the Atlantic and Gulf coasts of southern North America, the Caribbean, and Brazil. Other plantation areas were the deep, wide valleys in the tropical and subtropical regions of Mexico, Venezuela, Colombia, Ecuador, and Peru. The crops, of greater or lesser importance according to time and place, were sugar, cacao, tobacco, cotton, and coca. The plantation economy was already well defined by the beginning of the seventeenth century.[18] It had obvious implications for slavery and the general economy of the Spanish empie. In the sixteenth century the crown attempted to diversify the economy of its possessions by creating, besides mining, a craft industry connected with agriculture. It tried to increase the production of cochineal and woad, for example, but by the end of the century the policy was obviously a failure. From then on, the colonial economy basically relied on mining, but in the meantime in tropical areas on the Atlantic coast there had begun the production of export crops, which were highly successful in European markets but which were outside the sphere of Spanish control of market distribution. Tobacco, for exam-

[16] Vásquez de Espinoza, 1948.

[17] Feijoó, 1763.

[18] There is an abundant bibliography on the relationship of African slavery and the plantation economies. Among the more important works are the following: For Brazil, Taunay, 1939; Goulart, 1949; Cardoso, 1962; Westin de Cerqueira, 1967; Stein, 1970; and Galloway, 1971. For the Caribbean, Saco, 1937-44; Ortiz, 1947; Debien, 1955; Mintz, 1959; De Branche, Debien, *et al.*, 1960; Guerra y Sánchez, 1964; Moreno Fraginals, 1964; Klein, 1967; and Williams, 1970. For the Atlantic coasts of Venezuela and Colombia, there are many pertinent details in such documentary collections as Arcila Farías, 1950; *Materiales para el estudio de la cuestión agraria en Venezuela (1800-1830)*, 1964; Urueta, 1887-91; and Jaramillo Uribe, 1963. For the area covered by the Viceroyalty of Peru see Vásquez de Espinoza, 1948; Romero, 1949; and Feijoó, 1763.

ple, from the island of Margarita and from the coast of Tierra Firme did not develop as part of the trade between the Indies and Spain, but rather as a lucrative undertaking for Portugal and Holland. Both the latter were aided by the fact that they had part of the slave trade in their hands, and so could meet the needs of the planters in this respect. Such a situation clearly encouraged unofficial commercial exchange and the flow of contraband into the area. This trade was well developed by 1630.[19]

From the sixteenth century up to the second half of the nineteenth, those Latin American countries which had developed specialized plantation economies used slave labor almost exclusively. Sugar production is typical of a monocultural plantation economy. Except for a few short periods, the demand for sugar increased steadily for more than three centuries, and this demand was directly reflected in the growth in number of sugar mills and the rising numbers of slaves imported into the continent. In 1570 Brazil had 65 sugar mills operated by 3000 slaves. By 1590 there were 118 mills operated by 13,000 slaves, with a production of about 8000 short tons of refined sugar. The number of sugar mills continued to increase. By 1630 there were 166. Eventually production stabilized at about 31,000 short tons a year in the last decades of the seventeenth century.[20] In the non-Iberian colonies of the New World, the increase in production and the consequent increase in slave numbers were even more spectacular. At the beginning of the eighteenth century, documents presented to the British Parliament and the French Council of Commerce clearly testified that sugar was considered by the French and British to be the most important commercial product of their colonial possessions. In 1700 there were 400 sugar mills on the French islands of Guadeloupe, Martinique, and Haiti, with an annual production of approxiamtely 18,750 short tons of refined sugar. At the same time, the nineteen British colonies utilized 800,000 slaves to produce approximately 165,345 short tons a year.[21]

The above figures correspond to the mercantilist period

[19] H. and P. Chaunu, 1956-59, vol. VIII; Borah, 1945; and Berthe, 1960.

[20] This information is based on works cited in n. 18 above. See also Simonsen, 1937.

[21] This information is also derived from the studies listed in n. 18 above.

in the plantation economy when the demand for sugar and other tropical products in world markets, and also the pressures exerted by such an economy on the productivity of its slave labor force had not yet reached their maximum development. Correlating the above statistics of gross output with the longevity of the slave labor force is a difficult task. However, around the middle of the eighteenth century the average per capita productivity of the plantation slave fluctuated between 1250 and 1750 pounds of sugar a year. The average working life on the plantation was considered good if it reached a figure of fifteen years. The annual death rate of adult Negroes was approximately 5 percent. But from the second decade of the nineteenth century, the mercantilist commercial system, which had acted as a restraint on the productivity of the sugar colonies through a close control of their trade, gave way to the freer market forces of contemporary capitalism. As a consequence the demands on the slave labor force brutally increased. The required per capita production for each slave rose to 2500 pounds or more a year. The average working life fell to seven years, and the annual death rate of adult Negroes often exceeded 6 percent.[22]

The implications of such figures are manifestly brutal. The historical relationship of plantation economies and the institution of slavery cannot be considered other than a denial of life and dignity. This specific situation has come to epitomize both the condition of slavery in general and the existence of the Negro in Latin America, since other sectors of the slave population did survive without being submerged in this world of the plantation. The exact points of comparison between the various systems of captivity and the plantation economies have not yet been historically established, but they could only affirm the uselessness of discussing whether the institution of slavery was more humanitarian in the Portuguese, Spanish, French, Dutch, or English colonies; or of discussing possible exceptions in the sense of benevolence and mutual regard between masters and slaves. The economic link of plantation and slavery was simply too

[22] These figures are averages drawn from the sources, set out in n. 18. Other pertinent works are von Lippmann, 1941-42; Correia Lopes, 1944; and Taunay, 1941.

strong in the societies associated with it. It is clear that the
type of historical inquiry indicated would both substantiate
the irrelevancy of a greater or lesser degree of benevolence
and emphasize productivity as the fundamental determining
factor. In this regard, there are at least two major considerations. First, as the world market expanded and the demand
for plantation products developed, the treatment of slaves
became dehumanized. This was especially so in those countries where the slave trade lasted well into the nineteenth
century, and the process of abolition was the longest delayed.

In contrast to plantation societies the slaves' standard of
living was considerably better in regions where slavery was
not exclusively confined to agricultural production but was
associated with a wider range of economic and professional
activities. In these cases slavery was to some degree integrated into all sectors of society with the result that a variety
of types of slavery were present rather than one primary
type ordained by a plantation system of production. Blacks
in such societies could achieve, despite their status, a high
degree of prestige, if they were skilled artisans, if they were
domestic servants, or if they were related to the old colonial
families of the conquistadors. These situations were common
in the non-Caribbean areas of Spanish society, and to a lesser
degree in the Spanish Caribbean and in Brazil. This complex
social reality was not created simply by prolonged contact
between different ethnic groups with diverse cultural heri-
tages, but by the specific structure of the colonial economy.

Other Uses of Slave Labor

During the conquest of Spanish America, and in the years
immediately following, many of the leading conquistadors
and soldiers received encomiendas of Indians in recognition
of their services.[23] But encomiendas were not granted to all
the settlers. Not all of them had participated in the conquest,
and not all of them were considered to have contributed
signal services to the crown. But many of them needed labor
for their business ventures, assistants in their professions,

[23] See Introduction, n. 1; chap. 1, n. 17.

or servants in their homes. This situation was even more pressing in the non-Spanish colonies in the Caribbean, where the Indian population for all practical purposes was extinct by the beginning of the seventeenth century. The qualification to be made here is that most of the consumer goods and manufactured items useful to a tropical economy were imported into the Dutch, French, and English possessions, and to a lesser degree Brazil, directly from their respective homelands, utilizing wider maritime resources and a more open trade than did the Spanish. The result was that the percentage of slaves not engaged exclusively in tropical crop cultivation was very low.

Within the above qualification, it could be said that slavery was so institutionalized in America that there was virtually no one, including Indians, with sufficient funds who did not purchase one or more slaves, even when they were not immediately required. The following are the main social groups who required them.

1. Master craftsmen and tradesmen used large numbers of Negro slaves, especially in the construction of buildings, bridges, and roads. Many of the Negroes used in construction in due course gained their freedom and in turn became craftsmen.[24]

2. Religious orders bought slaves to serve in churches, convents, colleges, missions, or on their haciendas. The Jesuits became especially notable for the training in trades which they gave to the slaves in their farming ventures. These slaves, known specifically as the slaves of the Jesuits, became particularly valuable.[25]

3. Businessmen in the maritime and overland transport system used large numbers of Negro slaves in different ways, for instance, as teamsters and muleteers. No doubt relevant here were the many royal decrees and ordinances aimed at preventing the Indians being moved from the districts or provinces where they lived.

4. Royal officials in many different places and times purchased groups of slaves in the king's name for such public

---

[24] Harth-Terré, 1960; Harth-Terré and Márquez Abanto, 1961a and 1961b; Mellafe, 1959; Lockhart, 1968; Boxer, 1969a; and Stein, 1970.
[25] Concolorcorvo, 1942; and Ponce, 1967.

works as the construction and maintenance of fortifications and roads, the heavy work in dockyards, and to help with carrying loads in places of difficult access.

5. Many individuals who had some small income bought slaves in order to hire them out on a yearly, monthly, or daily basis. This form of investment in slaves seems to have been fairly common in Brazil. On the other hand, in Lima in the mid-eighteenth century, the charge for hiring a Negro was 15 silver pesos a month. A little later, in 1793, a businessman in Lima who had some small landholdings and a brick factory, and who was also a moneylender, hired out six slaves that he owned to the local royal mint at the rate of 5 reales a day for each slave. In the ten months in which they worked, discounting their expenses, which included hospitalization for one and the burial of another, the owner netted a sum of 794 silver pesos. This was at a time when slaves cost about 500 pesos.[26]

6. Many of the official colonial institutions, such as the cabildos and hospitals, found slaves useful for the heavier physical tasks or for such relatively specialized jobs as that of town criers or watchmen.

7. The Indians were able to possess slaves and did so, though the total number was comparatively small. There would seem to be two different ways by which they were acquired. The first was by a simple purchase of slaves by leading Indians who had become important economically and socially. In Peru they would include the descendants of the pre-conquest noble Inca families or of Indian provincial nobility. In addition there were the free Indians, or those unassigned to the encomienda system, who formed the quarter of El Cercado in Lima, many of whom had specialized trades. In their case the purchase required the presence or permission of the appropriate magistrate. Indians also acquired slaves by an interesting variant of simple purchase. It was done on a community basis rather than an individual one. From the final years of the sixteenth century, the Peruvian Indian communities were allocated tasks considered to be for the public good, both for themselves and the

[26] Eschwege, 1944; and also Archivo Nacional del Perú, Sección Notarial, Notario Francisco de Acuña, vol. 20.

other inhabitants of the region, for example, the building of bridges, roads, and churches. However, faced later with renewal of laws of forced public labor, under which manpower was diverted from local industries and mining, the Indian communities offered equivalent material and money in lieu of their work. In many places this money was used to purchase slaves who reverted to the ownership of the native communities once the work was done.[27]

Unproductive Slavery

In many Latin American cities in the last two centuries of the colonial period, and also in rural areas near lines of communication and around the Indian communities, there were groups of Negro slaves without fixed occupation or abode. There is a distinction to be made here. Those who had no definite legal, economic, or social status were usually termed vagabond. On the other hand, the cimarrones, or runaway slaves, often formed armed bands, which were frequently organized along lines derived ultimately from tribal origins. Their activities were punishable by law. Although the vagabonds and cimarrones were unproductive slaves, we are concerned here only with the small groups or individuals who in a short space of time, without loss of status or infringement of the law, passed from productive work to inactivity. Also to be included as unproductive is the large number of Negroes purchased for no other end than that of luxury, to serve simply as companions and as doormen or porters in private houses. Although many areas suffered a perennial shortage of slaves, the general tendency of colonial administrators and European and Creole settlers was to seek more and more slaves with the sole idea that an ample supply at lower prices would solve the major part of colonial economic problems. This idea appears to have received an increasing emphasis as the state and the economic structure of the empire gradually lost their capacity to control and channel the activities of large sections of colonial

[27] Harth-Terré, 1960; and Harth-Terré and Márquez Abanto, 1960b. See also n. 3 of this chapter.

society into active production. Such a situation was obvious from the second half of the seventeenth century onward.

The direct causes of unproductive slavery, apart from motives of ostentation or luxury, were the sudden discontinuance or transformation of some economic activity so that it no longer required as many slaves as it had originally. These changes occurred frequently and sometimes catastrophically, with the death of an entrepreneur, or with earthquakes, droughts, Indian rebellions, or the exhaustion of mining deposits. Many Spanish American cities became characterized by a large, inactive population, parasitic and idle. This situation raises such questions as how long slavery remained economical after Latin America developed from a mercantile system into that of modern capitalism, and what precise bearing uneconomical slavery had on the history of abolition.

The first comment to make in this respect is that the development of modern capitalism in the Latin American economy was not rapid, nor is it easy to ascribe precise chronological limits to it. It certainly did not occur in all the different regions at the same pace. A point that has been much discussed, for example, is whether it would be correct to say that by 1850 Brazil had entered an economic stage which could be defined as contemporary.[28] The answer could also be regarded as doubtful for the remaining Latin American countries. Certainly, however, by 1850 the characteristic features of the older mercantile system were no longer evident, and in many regions fundamental changes were occurring in monetary systems, with greater and quicker mobilization of capital and credit, and with changes in systems of production. Where production was still utilizing slavery, there was an evident crisis, and alternative methods of labor were being tried out. In many countries Negro slavery had in fact already disappeared somewhat before 1850. In general, slavery ended first in countries which did not rely on plantation economies and which at the same time had a large mestizo population to draw on for labor. This was true of the republics at the south of the continent,

[28] Freyre, 1970.

Uruguay, Argentina, and Chile. In Mexico at the end of the eighteenth century, it had been found that sugar mills could function successfully on the basis of a paid labor force. Clearly a change of this nature was largely if not wholly dependent on such related factors as the maximum utilization of the means of production, appropriate techniques, and the production of food or other goods which could form part of the payment for such work.[29] In Venezuela in 1835, after the slave trade had been virtually at a halt for a long period, but when slavery still existed as an institution, work on the coffee, cacao, and sugar plantations was being performed by paid labor. In contrast to Brazil, the coffee boom in Venezuela did not produce an internal movement of the remaining available slaves in the country, but had merely decreased the already extremely low wages paid to Negro workers, the children of slaves who were now free. By 1850, in no province of the country was there more than a 3 percent slave population. Most of the remaining slaves were about forty years old, at the end of their lives and their productivity. The infamous institution had become unproductive.[30]

The trend away from slavery and toward a paid labor force came in a different way in those countries or regions where a long relation between a plantation economy and slavery had not given rise to any significant nonslave population of workers. What is more, in these areas there were the extreme pressures of world demand for tropical products, together with the absolute dependence of these regions on international markets. If it is true to say that the idea of replacing slaves with paid workers was strong in some countries in the early decades of the nineteenth century, it is also true that in other countries economic circumstances strongly mitigated against it. It is in this sense that there was such a large gap between the ideal of abolition, with use of paid free workers, and its actual implementation. In Cuba as early as 1816, such intellectuals as Francisco de Arango had already broached the problem and insisted on the necessity of replacing slave labor. The crisis brought

[29] Bauer, 1967.
[30] Lombardi, 1969a, 1969b; and *Materiales para el estudio de la cuestión agraria en Venezuela (1800-1830)*, 1964.

about by the shortage of slaves in the 1830s caused others to stress the same idea—Antonio José Saco, well-known historian and patriot, among others.[31] Ultimately their ideas took hold: the slaves on the plantations were transformed into paid workers on the same plantations, much as had already been done to some extent in Venezuela and Colombia. But the point is that this change occurred only when it had become impossible to maintain and add to the number of Negro slaves necessary for the normal functioning and growth of the sugar mills. Thus slavery became unproductive here too, but only after a long period of twenty or thirty years, and when, already on the decline, it alternated with other forms of forced labor. From this point of view, the groups of Chinese and mestizo workers, taken on for periods of five, ten, or twenty years with wages—and retained afterwards on the basis of debts—were an important prerequisite to abolition. To all intents and purposes they were semi-slaves.[32]

[31] Arango y Parreño, 1952, vol. I; Saco, 1859 and 1928; Moreno Fraginals, 1964; and Corwin, 1967. For José Antonio Saco, see Introduction, above. Francisco de Arango (1765-1837), was well known for his work as a politician and economist, especially through his writings, being much interested in Cuban agriculture, and specifically the effects of sugar production.

[32] Moreno Fraginals, 1964. For another, though not necessarily a fundamentally different, point of view on unproductive slavery in relation to abolition of the trade and of slavery, see Graham, 1966.

CHAPTER FIVE

SLAVERY AND SOCIETY

Legislation, Relating to Slavery

The representatives of the Portuguese crown, the Spanish Council of the Indies, the royal high courts or audiencias, the local cabildos, the viceroys, and the governors were all constantly enacting legislation regulating the activities of Negro slaves. A copious body of laws and regulations was drawn up in a very short time covering the most varied, and frequently the most unexpected and intimate aspects of the life of the slaves. Documentary sources, together with associated private material, which is even more extensive, make it possible to reconstruct the details of their daily lives. Here it will only be possible to sum up the major tendencies shown by such sources.

In social legislation, there can be said to be three basic preoccupations on the part of the Spanish and Portuguese rulers in regard to both slaves and freedmen. The first was to prevent the Negroes from living together with the Indians, or from mixing with the Europeans. The second was to prevent slaves from escaping and becoming cimarrones, and to combat the activities of the cimarrones, all of which could be considered as implying a form of slave rebellion. The third motive was to change or channel unproductive and vagabond slaves into economically productive and socially acceptable activities. In a word, the two crowns attempted to maintain a strict social control, aimed at maximum economic yield and the preservation of a stratified, hierarchal society with a precise regulation of the relationship between master and slave.

The Iberian kingdoms had a long legal tradition of slavery, to which they added in the initial period of their American colonial experience. Such questions as the purchase and sale of slaves, legal ownership, succession upon the death of owners, the rights of slaves to buy their liberty, other forms of manumission, and penalties for those who ran away or who committed other felonies were far from being new legal experiences when they began to occur in the New World. The precedents were clear, and in a very general sense royal officials merely applied them in America, at least initially. New circumstances required substantial modifications and the enactment of further laws by the crown and the conquistadors. Such situations were brought about, for example, by large concentrations of slaves in certain parts of the continent, and also by the fact that various racial groups had to live side by side. Particularly important in this regard were the Indians. Other changes were made necessary by the large numbers of cimarrones and vagabond slaves in the colonies. Slavery certainly was no novelty in human society, but it was in America that it reached its maximum development.

Although the legal systems developed by Spain and Portugal often coincided, they sometimes differed. Neither empire had what could be described as a complete, formalized code of laws dealing with Negro slaves. The Spanish empire by 1580 had a body of laws and regulations sufficient for any and all circumstances, but in Brazil this was not done until the nineteenth century. The absolutism and centralism of the Hapsburgs were responsible for a whole series of administrative reforms which renovated, adapted, and extended the old medieval legislation of slavery. Viceroys, governors, royal audiencias, cabildos, chief magistrates, and lieutenant-governors not only had clearly defined powers but also had access to compilations of legal precedents, printed or handwritten, summarizing royal decrees, memoranda of agreements, and other documents which had been the result of the work of their predecessors.[1] There was very little of such codification

[1] Most of the basic laws concerned with both the treatment of slaves and their relationships with other racial groups can be consulted in Encinas, 1945, and in the *Recopilación de Leyes de las Indias*, 1943. There are other pertinent collections, some published and some not, of laws and ordinances received in the various agencies of government (offices of viceroy or governor, royal audiencias, or cabildos). The

in the Portuguese colonies. The feudal character of the early Portuguese occupation of Brazil caused power to become almost exclusively centered in the town councils, which were soon controlled by planters or mine owners according to the circumstances. It is from the town councils that almost all the slave laws and regulations came. The Spanish influence in Brazil between 1580 and 1640, and later the centralizing tendencies of enlightened despotism diminished somewhat this form of local power, but really caused little radical change in slave legislation. The town councils and local administrative officials, who in effect directly represented the interests ofthe major owners of the slave labor force, continued as before to pass laws and regulations concerning relationships between the various groups involved with slavery. In this way local circumstances and considerations were primary, but with frequent interventions by the royal government. These were often the result of petitions made or initiated by the bishops and archbishops of Rio de Janeiro and Salvador da Bahia. In 1711, for example, at their petition the crown attempted to create the office of solicitor, or judge of inquiry, specifically charged with investigating complaints of maltreatment and abuses on the part of owners. The attempt was unsuccessful.[2]

The Spanish rulers and officials of the crown were particularly concerned that the Africans and Indians should live in separate communities wherever possible. The motives were religious, moral, political, and were intended to protect the Indians. We have already pointed out that Levantine Negroes or Moslem slaves were not legally permitted to be imported. We also pointed out the status, and indeed notoriety, of many of the first slaves, who acted as auxiliaries and companions of the conquistadors. The abuses and ex-

---

memoranda and writs of agreement are other documents which are now difficult to find. Some of them are available in collections which have come from the audiencias. Among the historians who have studied this aspect of slavery may be cited Vial Correa, 1957; Mellafe, 1959; Jaramillo Uribe, 1963; and Lockhart, 1968.

[2] Published legislation on slaves and Negroes in Brazil can be found in such collections as *Codigo Filipino ou ordenações e leis do Reino de Portugal,* 1869-70, and *Actas de Câmara da Vila de São* Paulo, 1914-15. Also see Lahmeyer Lobo, 1962; Boxer, 1969a; and Prado, 1971.

For the centralizing tendencies of enlightened despotism, see, for example, the Marquis of Pombal (chap. 2, n. 38).

cesses committed by African born and Creole Negroes in the Indian villages and communities obliged the authorities to take measures which were given legal expression, for example, in a series of royal decrees in 1541, 1551, 1554, 1567, 1592, proclaimed in various parts of the New World. These stipulated that Negroes should not live in Indian villages, take Indians into their service, or have business dealings with them.[3]

However, the many laws enacted to protect the Indian villages and communities were only partially successful. Circumstances became complicated when these villages and their lands found themselves near population centers with a high percentage of Negroes, mulattoes, or mestizos with Negro blood. Other villages were bordered by large landed estates. The great haciendas based on cattle, other stock, or mixed agriculture in the Andean region, Mexico, the plains, or the pampas very seldom used the labor of slaves or of free Negroes or mulattoes. Such use occurred only in periods of increased market demand, which in fact were very few, or when new regions were opened up to agriculture. However, generally speaking, the large estates strongly resisted newcomers from the cities and mestizo villagers settling within their confines. Consequently the Indian villages came under particular pressure, especially in the seventeenth and eighteenth centuries, to incorporate individuals and families, often Negroes, into their numbers. Some of the chieftains contributed to the process by renting out community lands to mulattoes and free Negroes or by marrying off their daughters to them, with the ultimate result that there were a number of black mixed-bloods who had all the common privileges and rights of the remaining members of the Indian villages.[4] Censuses carried out in Indian districts and villages near the city of Córdoba in 1785 and 1792 showed quite clearly that there were a large number of Negroes and mulattoes among Indian families, who had even assimilated the characteristics of the native family structures. Some of

---

[3] Konetzke, 1953-62; Encinas, 1945; and *Recopilación de Leyes de las Indias*, 1943.

[4] Gibson, 1964; Mellafe, 1968; and Mörner, 1970a.

them were members and mayors of the village councils, the cabildos.[5]

The problems of relationships between Negroes and Indians, and between Negroes and Spaniards, appeared first in the Antilles, Panama, and Mexico. The measures tried there were then extended to the rest of the Spanish possessions, being modified to a greater or lesser degree according to circumstances. Since the difficulties in the beginning arose mainly in the towns, it was the cabildos that undertook the task of attempting to regulate the different racial groups living in relative proximity. All the cabildos in America enacted similar regulations which were contained in various ordinances designed for law enforcement and in other ordinances described simply as being for Negroes or slaves.[6] The regulations prohibited slaves from carrying arms, wandering at night without permission of their owners, going into the Indian markets, entering private property, cutting down trees, and engaging in commerce.

The one great problem, however, for the Spanish crown, the Council of the Indies, and the colonial administrators was the question of cimarrones, who not only rebelled against the authorities but often resorted to banditry, making armed attacks on the roads and against the villages. The cimarrón communities established in the jungle or in favorable geographical situations posed a constant threat to the authorities and to the established colonial settlements. The regions of tropical plantations, with their extensive open areas of cultivation, a limited European and Indian population and their location in places of difficult access and defense especially suffered from the cimarrones. In Peru it is clearly verifiable that the cimarrones increased their depredations at times of agricultural crises such as poor harvests and droughts.[7]

The escape of Negro slaves began fairly early in the New World. As early as 1520 in Cuba, the Licentiate Zuazo ordered that a number of slaves who had been hiding in the moun-

<hr>

[5] González and González de Mellafe, 1967.

[6] Mellafe, 1959; and *Libros del Cabildo de Lima*, 1935, vol. I. These documents were known as *ordenanzas de policía, fieles ejecutores, ordenanzas para negros,* or *ordenanzas para esclavos.*

[7] Mellafe, 1959.

tains were to be punished by being whipped and having their ears cut off. Attacks by cimarrones on Spanish and Indian villages and on travelers and pack trains on the main roads became common—in 1537 in Mexico, 1538 in Cuba, in 1546 in Hispaniola and northern Peru, in 1548 in Honduras, and in 1550 in Santa Marta and again in Peru.[8] Between 1555 and 1556 there was such a large uprising of slaves near Panama that the viceroy of Peru, the Marquis of Cañete, who was on his way to take up his post, had to negotiate an armistice with them. In 1572, the corsair Francis Drake, after having taken and sacked the city of Nombre de Dios, Panama, with the help of the cimarrones of the region then marched through the countryside attacking local haciendas. This action confirmed Spanish fears of the political potential of such slaves. It is beyond the scope of the present work to examine the finer points of the question of the cimarrones, despite the interest of the topic. They were a problem throughout the colonial period.[9]

Given the danger posed by the cimarrones, specific and severe ordinances concerning runaway Negro slaves were enacted by the governors and audiencias and sanctioned by the king. These ordinances were promulgated at different times and places according to necessity. Eventually, between 1571 and 1574, as a consequence of Drake's activities, the royal audiencia of Panama gathered together the various relevant provisions and royal decrees, and brought them up to date to form a complete body of laws on the subject. In 1680 these were incorporated in the Recopilación de las Leyes de los Reinos de Indias, constituting the definitive procedures to be taken against cimarrones.[10]

The laws can be summarized as follows: The expenses

---

[8] Saco, 1937-44; Sauer, 1966; and Lockhart, 1968. For Zuazo, see p. 13.

[9] There seems to be no general work dealing with the cimarrones, although a large number of regional studies have been made. Saco, 1937-44; and Guillot, 1961, have included the theme in their works. For Brazil consult Rodrigues, 1931; Pierson, 1942; Carneiro, 1946; and Prado, 1971. For Colombia see Escalante, 1954; Cardot, 1957; Salmoral, 1962; and Jaramillo Uribe, 1963. Cuba has been dealt with by Pérez de la Riva, 1946; Dalton, 1967; and Barnet, 1968. For Mexico see Querol y Roso, 1935; Corro, 1951; Davidson, 1966; Love, 1967; and Taylor, 1970. Carvalho Neto, 1965, has studied the theme in regard to Uruguay. For Venezuela consult Arcaya, 1949; Brito Figueroa, 1960; Acosta Saignes, 1961a; and Cardot, 1961.

[10] *The Spanish Law Code of the Indies of 1680* was the end result of a large

involved in the recapture of fugitive slaves were to be shared between the royal treasury and the individual interested parties. To this end special funds were created in many cities. Punishments to be meted out to runaways were stipulated. If a slave was absent for four days, he was to receive a total of fifty lashes. For eight days and a distance of a league (three miles) from the city, the punishment was one hundred lashes and an iron shackle of twelve pounds, on one foot for two months. If the slave fled for a period of less than four months outside the city, but without becoming involved with cimarrones, he would receive one hundred lashes for the first offense and banishment for the second. If he had joined the cimarrones, another hundred lashes was added. An absence of more than six months and the committing of some offense, whether or not with the cimarrones, was punishable by death.[11] Robbery, rape, and murder entailed extreme penalties, which varied according to region and time. Castration was common as a punishment up to the middle of the sixteenth century; mutiliation of body members and slow death also were inflicted in various forms.[12]

The new humanitarian morality of the Age of Enlightenment had various effects on slave legislation. Mainly through the influence of the monarchs and ministers of enlightened despotism in the Iberian peninsula in the second half of the eighteenth century, there came into being a strong ideological opposition to slavery. However it availed very little against

---

number of attempts to collect and codify the vast profusion of laws and ordinances applying to the New World. Some codifications had been efforts on a regional basis (e.g., the *Cedulario de Puga* [1563] for Mexico) while others, on a continental scale, had been unsuccessful or partially so (the *Código Ovandino* [1569-71]. Diego Encinas' *Cedulario Indiano* seems to have been the first corpus successfully published. It is useful in that it frequently contains the full text of what is sometimes fragmentary in the *Recopilación*. One of those involved in the groundwork that eventually led to the latter was Antonio de León Pinelo (see Introduction). Although the *Recopilación* was of general application, each province still retained its particular ordinances and statutes. Despite new efforts by the Bourbons (especially Charles III) for a code that would include their extensive legislation, the *Recopilación* continued to be the main legal code for the Spanish possessions during the rest of the colonial period. See Ots Capdequí, *Manual de historia del derecho español en Indias*, Buenos Aires, 1945.

[11] Encinas, 1945; *Recopilación*, 1943; Vial Correa, 1957; and Mellafe, 1959. Many of the ordinances enacted by the cabildos in the sixteenth century have been published. See, for example, Urueta, 1887-91, vol. II.

[12] See n. 11 above.

the practical situations, concrete economic interests, and increase in prejudice and segregation at the time. One of the architects of enlightened despotism was the Marquis of Pombal in Portugal, who promulgated a series of laws between 1761 and 1773 which not only removed the old invidious distinctions between Old and New Christians but also proclaimed liberty at birth for the offspring of Negro slaves then living in Portugal and freedom for any slaves henceforth brought into the country. For Brazil, Pombal introduced some important modifications in the treatment and control of slaves, especially in the gold-mining regions and in such others as Serro do Frio, where large numbers of slaves had been used since 1729 to obtain diamonds. Government officials of these regions were charged with carrying the new laws into effect. Later, the promulgation of the Código Criminal do Império do Brasil was a legal endeavor to suppress a number of cruel punishments, for example, the practice of placing a heavy iron shackle on the leg of a slave who had attempted to flee.[13]

However, like much of the reform legislation of the period, it was the result more of humanitarian pressures than a consideration of practical possibilities. The humanization of slave legislation in itself was very far from being enforceable on the plantations and in the mines. Many of Pombal's ordinances, for example, only served in the end to curtail what very little autonomy the Negroes had had in the mines. In the century that followed, slaves in Brazil were more badly treated and more completely segregated than ever before. Owners of the sugar plantations and mines, through the municipal councils, continued to set the norms of punishment according to whatever was most convenient to their interests.

The situation was similar, or perhaps even worse, in the Spanish colonies. The Código Negro promulgated by Charles IV in 1789 by royal decree caused such protests and opposition from slave owners in the tropical areas, especially Caracas, Havana, Bogotá, and Santo Domingo, that it had

---

[13] *Criminal Code of the Empire of Brazil.* See Section 2 of Bibliography under *Código Criminal de Império do Brasil*, 1830; Boxer, 1963; Lahmeyer Lobo, 1962; and Prado, 1971.

to be suspended in 1794.[14] Humanitarian opposition to slavery and the social realities of the Spanish possessions in the second half of the eighteenth and early nineteenth centuries simply had nothing in common. A succession of regional economic crises throughout Spanish America and a significant increase in numbers of white mestizos and Negroes created a large rootless population which inundated the roads and villages. Mine owners and planters had almost endless problems in trying to obtain all the slaves they needed, and yet they were not able, or they feared, to employ the floating, idle population, which turned to begging, pillage, and robbery. The slaves in the manufacturing industries and in the sugar plantations and mills, given the circumstances in which they lived and worked, revolted whenever they could and fled to unpopulated regions to join groups of vagabonds and bandits. Every important sugar estate at the time maintained an armed body of mestizos, not only for self-defense in case of attack from outside but also to deal with uprisings within the plantation. Order and control of a multiracial society, which had been the ideal of the absolute monarchs of the sixteenth century, and which they had partly succeeded in creating, fast disappeared in such circumstances. The state was now a weak entity, with power largely devolving upon the armed guards maintained by the major land and mine owners. Even the royal armies came to rely on them, especially in the provinces. And it is no coincidence that in many places free Negroes and first-generation mulattoes were excluded from the militia and regular army.[15]

In such an economic and social situation the number of cimarrones and their activities became endemic. In some places insurrections and attacks by armed bodies of slaves were frequent. In the region of Bahia, for example, there were conspiracies and revolts in 1800, 1809, 1813, 1816, 1826, 1828, 1830, and 1835.[16] In Venezuela in the second half of the eighteenth century, it was estimated that between 30,000 and 40,000 Negroes and mestizos were in a state of revolt. In its various provinces there were uprisings in 1732, 1749,

[14] Leal, 1961. *Código Negro: Black Slave Code.*
[15] Prado, 1971.
[16] Rodrigues, 1931; and Prado, 1971.

1751, 1755, 1760, 1765, 1770, 1771, 1774, 1776, 1786, 1787, 1789, 1790, 1794, 1795, 1798, and 1799.[17]

In the eighteenth and nineteenth centuries the *palenques* and *quilombos* of the cimarrones changed considerably from what they had been before (page 34). Often they evolved from small, fortified places hidden in inaccessible regions into villages with highly organized defense systems and extensive palisades and walls. They were no longer a refuge for a mere dozen or so fugitive Negroes and mulattoes, but came to count among their inhabitants the other races as well, frequently including a number of Creoles and even Europeans. More than being tribal groups attempting to follow forms derived from their African origins, they developed sophisticated political and military organizations patterned on those of the established colonial urban centers. There was also a strong religious mixture or fusion within the *palenques*, which became more and more combined with messianic forms of religion.[18]

It is easy to understand how the attempts to humanize slavery came to nothing, and how on the contrary new legislation and regulations were created to combat the problem of the cimarrones. To this end royal decrees for the Spanish colonies were published in 1796, 1820, and 1824. Greater care was given the legislation on the matter of recapture, since the scarcity of black slave labor was seriously affecting tropical production in those areas still under Spanish rule.[19] Colonial administration and justice attempted to control and mitigate the economic and social effects of unproductive slavery in its various forms. Besides the cimarrones, there were large numbers of slaves who in various ways legally obtained their freedom and who came to swell the ranks of free, paid workers or simply became vagabonds. These legally free, enfranchised slaves, as they were known, were considered subjects of the Spanish crown, and they were entitled to all the rights and obligations that this status implied. They were liable to a poll tax or tribute paid as recognition of the relationship of subject and state, similar

[17] Brito Figueroa, 1960; and Acosta Saignes, 1962.
[18] See the studies indicated in n. 9 of the present chapter. See also Bastide, 1967.
[19] Corwin, 1967; and Dalton, 1967.

to that paid by the Indians, which in the sixteenth century amounted to 12 reales a years, but which was very much resisted and never widely collected.[20]

Measures of two types were taken by the state against unproductive slavery and vagabond slaves because of their relationship with the economic and social crises of the period and even with problems of internal and external security. Direct measures were enacted by institutions of government in each region from the earliest times of colonial administration. They prescribed that every Negro, slave or free, had to live with a master or owner of a business or had to have some occupation, trade, or known dwelling place. Relaxation in the enforcement of these provisions was frequently referred to by those who had business interests requiring the labor of such Negroes. One example is a petition presented to the viceroy by mine owners in Mexico in 1601 seeking to compel Negroes, those of mixed Indian and chino stock, and free mulattoes to work in the mines.[21] Measures of the second type were indirect. Among the most notable was the creation in the early seventeenth century of armed companies comprising free Negroes and mulattoes. This seems to have been one of the more successful partial solutions adopted by the crown in order to have some use and some control of the increasing numbers of unproductive Negroes. These companies from their inception became progressively more important as the state became less capable of maintaining a royal army sufficient to defend all the colonies, and as the structures of social control became weaker, at least in comparison with the previous century.[22]

Those responsible for colonial administration realized very early in the period of the conquest the basic function of statistics and registers in any system of social control and order. None of the above measures could have been effective if it had not been known how many Negroes there were in every region and city, how they lived, and what they produced. For this reason the cabildos were made responsible

[20] Konetzke, 1953-62.
[21] Information and examples on attempts to control vagabonds in the Spanish possessions can be found in Konetzke, 1953-62; N. Martin, 1957; and Corwin, 1967. For Brazil, see Boxer, 1969a.
[22] *Recopilación*, 1943; Konetzke, 1953-62; Lahmeyer Lobo, 1962; and Prado, 1971.

for carrying out counts of the servant population in the cities, and the parish priests for keeping separate parish registers of births, deaths, and marriages, in accordance with the different races and interracial groups of their parishioners. Later the royal audiencias, chief magistrates, inspectors of mines, and other officials received quite specific instructions on this point. This policy was intensified when unproductive slavery, manumission or enfranchisement, and the numbers of vagabond slaves and cimarrones became endemic problems. Owners were then required to declare the number of slaves they had and where, and to report, under severe penalty, cases of escape and crime.[23]

At the same time, police ordinances were brought up to date in regard to old provisions which forbade the sale of alcohol to Negroes, and regulated gambling and dancing. In some places an attempt was made to group free Negroes in villages with autonomous administration, and to control their movements by means of certificates which specified who they were owned by or working for.[24] For its part, the Catholic Church, one of the strongest institutions for social control, made particular efforts at the time in its work of evangelization among the slaves, creating a proliferation of confraternities or sodalities comprised of Negroes and mulattoes in all the important parishes. In Lima in the middle of the seventeenth century there existed eighteen such sodalities. They became an important social institution and an element of social stability in the period. They channeled the leisure time and any idleness of the Negro racial groups into recreational activities allowing scope for cultural forms of expression ultimately derived from Africa.[25]

The Interracial Caste System
Every society utilizing slavery must of necessity be highly stratified in order to exist. Spain and Portugal created such

[23] The gathering of demographic information had not only the aims of social control and order, but also clearly involved tribute, taxes, wages, etc. See Mellafe, 1967 and 1972. Some of the relevant documents have been published; see, for example, Apolant, 1968. Also useful are Harth-Terré, 1965; Mellafe, 1967; and Love, 1971.

[24] Urueta, 1887-91, vol. I; Archivo Nacional del Perú, Sección Histórica, Esclavos, Legajo 1; and Biblioteca Municipal de Lima, Cedulario del Cabildo, vols, I, V, VIII, and XIII.

[25] Castillo, 1925; Ovalle, 1888; and Bastide, 1967.

societies in the New World, and they attempted to justify them on the grounds of religion, tutelary responsibility, aristocracy, and good government. The ideal of Spanish social policy was that members of the various races, European, Indian, and African, should marry only within their race. In this way there would be a clearly defined social structure comprising the three groups: a white Spanish minority exercising economic and political control, a large Indian population, and an extensive body of slaves on the lowest level—objects of discrimination because of their obscure and heathen origins. In reality this segregation did not occur. There was a mixture of the three groups from top to bottom, forming as it were a whole complex of what the Spaniards called castes. The causes were many. The Spaniards themselves were actively involved in such mixing in different ways throughout three centuries. Their sexual unions, legitimate or otherwise, tended to be with Indian and Negro women in the sixteenth century; in the seventeenth with mestizo women with Indian, Spanish and African blood; and in the eighteenth almost exclusively with European—mestizo, or white mestizo women, that is to say with women of mixed blood, of Indian, and a predominantly white ancestry.[26] In the sixteenth century, in the period of the conquest, the separation of the main groups remained more or less clear. The only significant exceptions were the rights and privileges normally associated with whites which were conceded to groups of Indian nobles or chieftains, and those granted to Negroes who had helped with the conquest itself. But in the last decades of the century and the early years of the following century, there developed a complicated caste nomenclature.

The relationships between Negroes and Europeans in the Portuguese possessions of the New World were much freer, and less subject to legal constraints. This was especially true of the concubinage practiced by white owners with black and mulatto slave women. However, the customary informality characteristic of personal relations in Brazil was not evident in the rigid stratification of society on the basis of

[26] See chap. 1.

112

color. The exercise of power was the privilege of whites. Segregation and violence were most common in precisely those areas where everyday human relationships appeared most liberal. What is more, this duality produced in the whites forms of reaction with complex psychological and social implications which, in effect, have survived to the present time.[27] The fact that such apparent liberality was largely restricted to extramarital sexual relations has many points pertinent to the theme of racial intermixing.

There are a number of earlier historical factors which are relevant. More than a century of exploration and expansion previous to their experience in Brazil brought the Portuguese into contact with opulent and polygamous societies, where not only did they become politically and economically dominant but where power and social prestige encouraged concubinage. Portuguese migration from the Old to the New World included relatively fewer European women, and they came later than did the Spanish women. The type of Indian society which the Portuguese encountered was, in general, far less advanced and more warlike, resulting in less race mixture with the Indians than between Negro slaves and white masters. Thus marriage between the Portuguese and Indian women as a means of political alliance between the invader and the native elites did not occur in Brazil as it occurred with the Spaniards in Mexico and Peru.[28] Thus the most significant group of mixed bloods in Brazil, numerically and socially, was the mulatto, the union of black and white, rather than the mestizo of white and Indian ancestry, or people of black and Indian descent more characteristic of Spanish America. Of course, all possibilities and mixtures of groups and subgroups did occur there.

In the nomenclature of the colonies, at the very bottom of the social scale were the "bad castes" or the "bad races," those of greatest color pigmentation, the pure Negroes. As the white minority groups became more aware of the impossibility of avoiding the proliferation of castes of mixed color and their movement upward in the social scale, so they

---

[27] Pierson, 1942; Ianni, 1962; Boxer, 1963; and Freyre, 1966.
[28] González and Mellafe, 1965.

intensified discriminatory measures and attempts at segregation. Although the restrictions affected all who were not Europeans, it was undoubtedly the Negroes and those with Negro blood, the people of "broken color," who encountered the worst discrimination, being isolated as they were from any possibility of social good standing, of positions of responsibility, of partaking in the most productive activities, and often of participating in religious and cultural life. Some of the restrictions have been mentioned, but there were many more, including stipulations as to type of clothing and food, regulations preventing low-caste persons from becoming master craftsmen in many trades, and even a prohibition against the use of coffins, which were to be used only by the Spaniards.[29]

The Basic Terminology of Race Mixture in Colonial Spanish and Portuguese America

	Indian (Mongoloid)	Black (Negroid)	White (Caucasian)
Primary Mixtures	mestizo (Indian-White)	pardo, zambo* (Indian-Black)	mulato (Black-White)
Secondary Mixtures	Indian	Black	White
Mestizo	mestizo	mestizo prieto	mestizo
Pardo, Zambo	mulato lobo indio alobado	mulato prieto pardavasco (Braz.)	——
Mulato	——	——	mulato morisco brancarão (Brazil)
Tertiary Mixtures	Mestizo		
Pardo, Zambo	mestizo pardo coyote (Mexico)		

* Also called in Spanish America: cochos, cambujos, chinos, jorochos, loros; in Portuguese America: cabaré, cafuso, cariboca, curiboca.

[29] Abundant work has been done on interracial mixture and groups in Latin America, and most of the studies mentioned in the previous notes to this chapter

114

The various categories of racial mixtures involving Negroes were numerous (see accompanying chart). The following can only include the broader, more general distinctions. The two most important groups were the mulattoes, implying a variable percentage of black and white blood, and the *zambos* or *pardos*, implying a mixture of black and Indian blood. The white mulatto meant the even mixture of white and black. The term *mulato morisco* or simply *morisco* (*brancarão* in Brazil) was applied to quadroons, the result of the union between men of European descent and white mulatto women. (The morisco mulattoes are not to be confused with the Moslem slaves imported into Spain and Portugal from North Africa who, in the sixteenth century, were also widely known as moriscos.) The morisco mulatto was frequently blond with blue eyes, and tended to pass as a European-Indian mixture or as Spanish or Portuguese, being often taken as such in the eighteenth century. The "dark" mulatto, the *mulato prieto*, or *pardavasco* in Brazil, was the offspring of a Negro and a woman of pardo blood. Three-quarters Negro, the prietos were dark enough to be taken frequently as full-blooded Negroes.

The zambos or pardos, who came from the union of Negroes with Indian women, were more common to the Spanish colonies. According to the color of the skin many groups were distinguished by names which varied somewhat from place to place (*cochos, cambujos, chinos, jorochos, loros,* etc). The most important were the *mulatos lobos* or *lobos*, who were the result of the union between Indians and pardos; and *alobados* or *indioş alobados*, that is, persons to all intents and purposes Indians but with some Negro admixture. Though crosses involving Negroes and Indians were more common in the Spanish possessions, they were by no means absent in the Portuguese American colonies. Many terms in different regions testify to the fact; *cabaré, cafuso, cariboca,* and *curiboca*. There are other terms, like *cabra,*

are relevant. A good critical review of the problem is Mörner, 1966. For general studies see Pérez de Barradas, 1948; Rosenblat, 1954; and Mörner, 1956, 1967, and 1970a. For Argentina, consult Endrek, 1966 and 1967. For Colombia, Jaramillo Uribe, 1967, is useful. For Mexico, see Roncal, 1944; and Aguirre Beltrán, 1946. Harth-Terré, 1965; Gutiérrez Seco, 1965; and Romero, 1965, can be consulted for Peru. For Uruguay, see Pereda Valdés, 1937 and 1940.

which indicated some vague percentage of white blood as well as Negro and Indian blood.[30] The word mestizo when used without any other qualification was taken in the colonies to mean the cross between white and Indian. Creole, *criollo*, was applied to people of completely European appearance born in the colonies. The combination of mestizos with Negroes or mulattoes gave rise to another whole series of subgroups. Among the most important was the dark mestizo, the *mestizo prieto*, who was the offspring of a mestizo as such and a Negro woman, and who was frequently confused with a mulatto. Also to be included is the *mestizo pardo*, or in Mexico *coyote*, who was the offspring of the white mestizo and a woman of pardo blood.[31]

Interbreeding and Manumission

Clearly the distinctions of color were both fine-drawn and complex. The Spaniards, especially, insisted on such distinctions as the castes threatened to cross the limits of racial and social stratification set in official policy. In the eighteenth century, the terminology described was in common use in the Spanish possessions with slight regional variations. In the Viceroyalty of Peru particularly, specific terms were used to indicate the proportions of Negro ancestry (*cuarterón* for quarter, *tercerón* for a third generation black descendent —an octaroon) and also the successive generations which had passed since the stock was purely Negro. There were other more elaborate classifications of racial types which can be said to be merely theoretical; that is, they were intended to be ethnographic and accompanied by illustrations of the typical dress of each caste. Extravagant racial classifications were very typical of the nineteenth century; those, for example, made by Riva Palacio, which have given rise to various historical studies, had in fact very little basis in social reality. Gonzalo Aguirre Beltrán is quite correct when he

[30] Perhaps it should be made clear that the expression *zambo* ("sambo") has no pejorative connotations in Latin America. The word *pardo* was frequently used vaguely by both the Spaniards and Portuguese to designate what has been more precisely defined above as mulatto. The Portuguese also used the term *mameluco* to describe a person of Negro and Indian blood or of white and Indian blood.

[31] Aguirre Beltrán, 1946; Rosenblat, 1954; and Love, 1971.

affirms that many curious and even humorous names applied to these castes were not used by inhabitants or authorities in the period.[32]

The most important castes, numerically speaking, were not the Negroes or the mulattoes or the pardos as such in the Spanish possessions, but rather their subgroups. In other words, the general tendency was to move continuously into the proliferation of the intermediate groupings. This applied particularly to the Negroes, quite apart from whether they were slave or free. Various causes, operating gradually over a length of time, were responsible for this. Royal decrees in 1526 and 1541 made it clear that the offspring of slaves were *not* to be considered as free, "despite being against the laws of the kingdom (Castile)"—the latter laws, in fact, having provisions in the opposite sense. The enactment of the above decrees made it advantageous to owners for slave women to bear children. This meant that slavery by birth in America was especially linked to the maternal line. The owners would often marry off their male Negro slaves with Indian women, and in such cases these decrees would be interpreted as inapplicable in that not only was the father held to be a slave, but also the mother. But, on the other hand, if a slave woman, married or otherwise, gave birth, it was taken that the children were slave irrespective of whether the father was free and of the caste to which he belonged.

In spite of the fact that royal decrees in 1527 and 1551 stipulated that every means was to be taken to ensure that Negroes were to marry only Negroes and to avoid sexual liaisons between slaves and Indian women, precisely the opposite occurred. On the one hand, the proportion of men and women shipped from Africa was very unequal. Up to 1640 at least, approximately one-third of the slaves imported were women. These slave women tended to become sexually involved with Spaniards or white mestizos. On their part

---

[32] Examples are *tente en el aire* ("hold yourself in the air," "stay in the air"), *no te entiendo* ("I don't understand you"), and *torna atrás* ("turn back"). Research undertaken by the author in the archives of Mexico, Colombia, Ecuador, Peru, and Chile has not yet come across any trace of such names. See the works indicated in n. 29 above, including Aguirre Beltrán.

was their interest that their children should not be slaves; the custom was that owners gave freedom to the children they had fathered on their slave women. Even the laws of the Indies made the point that a father was to have preference in the purchase of a slave who was his child.[33] Thus the only possibility that was often left to the male Negro for sexual union was with women who were Indian or colored mestizos. In fact, such unions were well accepted by the colonial encomenderos and entrepreneurs. Even though the offspring were not legally slaves, they could be taxed as Indians by the encomendero and added to the labor force under his control.

In Spanish America, then, successive racial intermixing involving individuals originally Negro with people of predominantly Indian or white descent was a common practice which transformed the black population into one of mixed bloods. There was a general preference to be of mestizo or white appearance as a means of coming closer to the social status of the European. Besides racial intermixture and the absorption of European culture, even to the point of imitating dress and speech, there was also an economic factor. A white mulatto or a morisco, for example, could often be registered as a European, or more commonly as a Creole, on baptismal records or in census surveys in the various suburbs or parishes, but this step meant bribing whoever was in charge. Another means was simply to purchase the title of white by means of the payment of a substantial sum to the central authorities.[34] Not only was the desire to be considered white a factor contributing to racial intermixture, but also the desire to be considered Indian, especially in the eighteenth century, although in the earlier periods in many places in America, it was often preferable to be a slave. The fact is that free mulattoes and zambos were usually required to pay a higher poll tax than were the Indians. The Indians also had other exemptions and rights, especially in the use of the land, which the colored mestizos could obtain only by purchase.

[33] *Recopilación*, 1943.
[34] Called *gracias al sacar*. See the works cited in n. 29 above. Consult also King, 1951.

As important to the Negroes and mulattoes as the whitening process outlined above were the ways and means of obtaining freedom. These were the subject of an extensive series of laws both in medieval Iberian and colonial legislation. There were two main ways in which manumission, or enfranchisement,[35] as it was more commonly known in the Spanish colonies, could be achieved: by the purchase of liberty by the slave himself, or by the conditions of a last will and testament. In the case of purchase, there would exist a prior agreement between owner and slave, or a legal representative of the latter. Such agreements were not necessarily based entirely on payment made by the slave for himself, but frequently involved the performance of certain work, such as going with the owner on a voyage or hazardous expedition. What was known as an agreement of enfranchisement was drawn up before a notary public, the conditions accepted by both parties clearly stated. A number of cases are known in the Spanish colonies in which owners were obliged by law, as retribution for some crime committed against the slave, to sign such an agreement. It was much more common for the slave to find some third person who was prepared to pay for his liberty, as the legal documents of the time put it, "for having done me a good turn." On such occasions there existed a written agreement between the benefactor and the owner. Common examples of these cases were of a father buying the liberty of his son, or a husband that of his wife.[36]

Economic circumstances in the various regions had a direct relationship with increase in numbers of enfranchised or ex-slaves. Such frequent, regional economic crises as changes in markets, mines becoming unproductive, and long periods of bad harvests or droughts often caused owners to have appreciable surpluses of slaves without useful work. Normally such slaves would be sold in other areas where labor was in demand, but many slaves were given freedom after some sort of compensation had been determined. In the Spanish

[35] The technical term here was *ahorramiento*.
[36] There are numerous examples in the Colecciones Notariales (records of the notaries public) in the national archives of many of the Latin American countries. See Section 1 of the Bibliography.

Caribbean area, especially Cuba, in the eighteenth century, there was such a short supply of slaves that real manumission was evaded by the creation of forms of semi-slavery.[37] The right of a slave to purchase his freedom was undermined by his having further obligations to a former master even when free. The most common way by which slaves obtained their freedom was through conditions stated in a will. It was very frequent to find in the testaments of wealthy persons possessing many slaves instructions freeing one or several of them. Varying reasons were given: the slave having been a good and faithful servant, motives of conscience or religion, the slave being a son or cases in which there were suspicions of paternity, or some other type of blood relationship.[38]

Interracial Antagonism and Restrictions on Marriage

It is clear that interracial relationships varied greatly throughout the colonial period in the New World. Manifestly both the white and Negro groups adopted defensive and antagonistic attitudes toward each other, while the large intermediate group of mestizos, involved as they were in a gradual whitening process, were in a more or less neutral position. Putting aside the period when the Negro acted as an ally in the Spanish conquest in America, it is possible to isolate various attitudes on the part of the slave toward white society. These generally comprised alliances of convenience and many forms of attack. They were fundamentally reactions to the oppression created by a social system that extensively exploited slaves for its own ends. Such reactions varied from the unconscious or partially conscious to the completely premeditated. Among the unconscious or partially conscious reactions could be included resigned servility, concubinage, and a number of circumstances associated with baptism and marriage. The latter refers to the special rela-

---

[37] Semi-slavery will be dealt with in chap. 6. More details on compulsory purchase of freedom, which may not necessarily concur with the above interpretation, can be found in Klein, 1967; and Corwin, 1967.

[38] It is common to find such cases in wills and testaments preserved in the Colecciones Notariales mentioned in n. 36.

tionship held to exist between sponsors and those sponsored by them in the celebration of both sacraments. This was of particular importance in Spanish America and in the social context of the period. In Lima, for example, in the sixteenth century, enslaved and free Negroes and mulattoes far preferred sponsors who were not only free but of a much higher social and economic status. It seems reasonable to assume that a similar preference existed in most of the major colonial cities, and that the cumulative effect, generation after generation, would eventually be to form, as it were, a social and psychological protective barrier for a large percentage of slaves and colored mestizos in the urban centers.[39] Also relevant is the social and political good standing attained by many Negroes and mulattoes in Indian and mestizo communities—a point already made.

The consciously defensive and often antagonistic reaction was represented by vagabond slaves and the cimarrones. At certain times the regional concentration of cimarrones suggested a war between castes, although in fact this never took clear form. The violence brought about by the Wars of Independence over two decades had the effect of absorbing what could have become a savage caste war. In many of the military campaigns of Independence, the Negroes, mulattoes, zambos, and other Negro admixtures in the armies were responsible for episodes very similar to those of the cimarrones, especially in the regions of La Plata and Gran Colombia. The same situation occurred many years later in Cuba.[40] The political and economic situation in the Caribbean in the first decades of the nineteenth century and the influence of the Negro revolution in Haiti were responsible for a number of slave conspiracies and uprisings in both Cuba and Santo Dimingo. They likewise were different from the traditional form of the cimarrón revolts, but on the other hand they failed to achieve any conscious unification of political and racial motives.[41]

Independence and the period of regional leaders or military bosses, the *caudillos*, largely changed the old colonial legal

[39] Mellafe, Poblete, and Manzur, 1967.
[40] Sales de Bohigas, 1970; and Barnet, 1968.
[41] Díaz Soler, 1953; James, 1963; and Corwin, 1967.

system in regard to segregation. Hitherto unknown ways for new groups to move up the social scale became open. In places like Venezuela the problem of the cimarrones, which had particularly and persistently plagued it, almost entirely disappeared by 1830, the escape of slaves becoming isolated and individual incidents.[42] Banditry, which became so common around the middle of the century in all the Latin American republics, had very different racial, economic, and political characteristics and little, if any, relationship with the old problem of cimarrones.

The numerous slave rebellions of the eighteenth century, the movement of groups who had originally been Negro into the whiter sectors of the social scale, and finally the danger which large masses of Negro slaves could pose in the political movements for independence all produced a significant increase in systems and methods of segregation. This increase occurred especially in those areas which relied most heavily on slaves for production, specifically, Brazil. There, given the special characteristics of its legal and institutional systems, the planters and mine owners were quite easily able to intensify segregation, since they were completely dominant at the provincial level. Similar defensive efforts by white groups occurred in the Spanish tropical colonies, although here they tended to be couched, and legally sanctioned, in the form of new laws, edicts, and provisions for the entire colony. The repeal of the more humanitarian laws which had been promulgated in 1789 was not sufficient for these white groups. The circumstances created by the Wars of Independence gave rise to further regulations on a more regional basis, reviving old drastic penalties and precautions of the Spanish colonies which had been forgotten or had been abolished by various codes in the seventeenth century. One such example was the Reglamento de Esclavos, enacted by the Governor of Puerto Rico, Miguel de la Torre, in 1826.[43]

This renewal of extreme, stringent laws also included measures designed to check interbreeding between the castes.

[42] Lombardi, 1969a. As is noted in chap. 6, Venezuela declared manumission in 1821, but as late as 1837 there were still almost 38,000 slaves in the country.

[43] Díaz Soler, 1953. For the laws of 1789, see pp. 107-108

It represented the revival of the old ideal, which had failed in the sixteenth century, of a pyramidal social structure maintained by marriages confined within the major racial groups. In 1778 a royal ordinance "to prevent the abuse of contracting unequal marriages" began to be extensively applied. This gave parents the right to control whom their offspring were to marry up to the age of twenty-five. But, since the Negroes, mulattoes, *coyotes*, and other Negro admixtures were not covered by the ordinance, it meant that the white or the very nearly white mestizo parents had sole control over the formation of family groups with claims to being white. A later royal decree in 1803 fixed the age limit at twenty-three years for men and twenty-five for women. Finally, another decree, in 1805, stipulated that all interracial marriages were to be approved by the civil authorities.[44] This gave the white groups much firmer control over interracial marriage than had ever been possible with the ecclesiastical authorities, who had been frequently accused of being too soft. Very often the reasons of conscience which the clergy adduced to justify such marriages covered concubinage, the existence of illegitimate children, abductions, and rape. The very fact that these situations occurred implied a way of life which the white elites regarded as their own exclusive prerogative, and which involved a manifest double morality leading to the enactment of such laws as the above.[45]

[44] Some of these stipulations have been published in Konetzke, 1953-62, vol. III. Comments on them, which may well vary from those expressed here, have been included in Corwin, 1967; Klein, 1967; and Martínez Alier, 1971.
[45] Interesting conclusions on this point are expressed by Martínez Alier, 1971.

CHAPTER SIX

ABOLITION AND ALTERNATIVES TO SLAVERY

Growth of the Mestizo Population

The growth of Negro slavery in Latin America varied according to place, time, and motive. Some regions, for example the Caribbean, reqired slaves from the conquest until well into the nineteenth century. In others, like Mexico and Chile, the greatest demand for slaves and the most active trade in them seem to have been around the middle of the seventeenth century. In the Viceroyalty of Peru, demand was greatest in the early part of the eighteenth century; and in the Plata region, Venezuela, and Colombia, in the last decades of that century. The Portuguese colonies in America imported more slaves in the eighteenth century than they did in all the other years the trade was operative there. Most of the nearly two million slaves shipped into Brazil at that time were in fact imported in the interval between 1761 and 1810. And most of those brought into the country during the nineteenth century were imported in the first forty years.[1]

Variations in the need for Negro labor in the different regions were caused by many circumstances: economic, demographic, and social. Changes in the economic base of a particular province could be responsible for the appearance or disappearance of slavery; in other regions, slavery as a means of production could become more of a hindrance than

[1] Goulart, 1949; and Curtin, 1969.

an advantage in comparison with the paid worker. However, around the time of Independence or a little later, regions which had not come to rely on slavery for production were very much the exception. Moreover, the fact that a particular region had passed its peak period of economic growth did not imply the absolute decline of slavery. Where there still existed a plantation economy, there likewise existed a continuing need for slaves; and it was no coincidence that these two factors occurred in precisely those regions where the Indian population was either very small when the Europeans came or had been annihilated in the early years of the occupation. In other words, slavery was still useful in areas where there was no large class of mestizos capable of replacing slaves as a paid labor force. The mestizos were in fact one of the major factors in the decline of Negro slavery in Spanish America. The earlier the mestizos appeared in significant numbers, and were included in active production, the sooner it became obvious how expensive slave labor was in comparison with free labor in the form of day laborers, tenant farmers, or miners.

At present it is virtually impossible to determine the proportion of mestizos at various periods in the Spanish and Portuguese American possessions, particularly colored mestizos, given racial interbreeding and dispersion. It is, however, possible to make only general observations. In the previous chapter, it was made clear that the Negro slave was likely to lose his racial characteristics by the second or third generation after arrival in America. This meant that the pure Negro population tended to be relatively small, with some local exceptions, while the colored mestizos became more and more numerous, despite the gradual whitening process and racial dispersion that this implied. From the middle of the sixteenth century in Mexico, for example, the mestizos of various types increased constantly and the pure Indian population decreased, whereas the numbers of pure Africans and Europeans remained steady. In 1810 there were some 10,000 pure Negroes as against approximately 620,000 colored mestizos, leaving aside others involved in further racial mixing with other groups. The Europeans represented 0.2 percent of the total population; the pure Negroes only 0.1

125

percent; Indians 60 percent; the white mestizos 17.9 percent; Indian mestizos 11.5 percent; and colored or African mestizos 10.1 percent. In other words, Mexico, a little before its political independence was a country with a very large mestizo population which was a potential substitute for slave labor.[2]

Similar situations occurred in the remaining Spanish American colonies, with variations as to the actual racial mixtures. Venezuela, which had had a large and constant influx of Negroes and where the Indian population had been almost completely wiped out in the initial century of European occupation, had in 1810 a population of whites and white mestizos of 20.3 percent, of Indians and Indian mestizos of 18.4 percent, and of Negroes and others with Negro blood of 61.3 percent.[3]

Chile, on the other hand, in the eighteenth century was mainly a province through which contraband slaves passed from Argentina to Peru and Upper Peru. It had very few Negroes, and these were largely concentrated in the mining areas and in the few irrigated valleys of the north. Elsewhere in the province the haciendas which ran stock or grew wheat or which were of mixed production were able to get ample labor from among the Indians and mestizos—a thoroughly mixed population with very few of pure blood. In 1778, the diocese of Santiago, that is to say the northern half of the country where 90 percent of the Negro slaves were concentrated, had a population of 241,313 of whom only 9 percent were listed as Negroes and mulattoes.[4] Cuba and Brazil, which received large shipments of slaves at the end of the eighteenth and in the nineteenth century, somewhat changed their racial composition in comparison with that of the rest of Latin America. For many years the total number of Negroes and mulattoes was on the verge of overtaking the

---

[2] Aguirre Beltrán, 1946, on the Negro population of Mexico. See also the studies of both Borah and Cook cited in the Bibliography on the Indian population.

[3] Brito Figueroa, 1961; and Rosenblat, 1954.

[4] Archivo Nacional de Santiago de Chile, Colección Fondo Antiguo, vol. 24, pieza 4. The confused way in which this census was recorded makes it impossible to calculate the approximate percentages of the remaining interracial groups. However, it is clear that a large number of mestizos with predominantly white appearance were counted as Spanish, the latter category thus composing 75 percent of the total population.

white population, whereas the groups of mestizos with Negro blood acquired three or four generations back were a lesser number. For example, in Cuba in 1795, the population to all intents and purposes could be divided into three groups: 49 percent were whites or white mestizos, 34 percent were Negroes, and 17 percent mulattoes.[5]

The growth of the mestizo population in Spanish America is both clear and significant. Around 1650, when the rapid decrease of the native population was still occurring on the continent, the number of mestizos was already greater than that of either the whites or the pure Negroes. The mestizos were at the time between 8 and 10 percent of the total colonial population. At Independence the purely Negro population in Spanish America must have been between 12 and 15 percent of the total, whereas the castes must have been between 30 and 35 percent.[6] When the wars of the period interrupted the regular shipment of slaves into America, the mestizo population was in a preeminent position to replace them. Free mestizos had not replaced Negro slaves before because a system based partly on slavery could hardly have been abolished without severe economic collapse, since the slave trade was not only central to the system but also an important factor in international diplomacy. Furthermore, the groups which were to provide labor in place of slaves had in fact been very little under effective governmental control or of effective use in the colonial economy.

Great Britain and Abolition of the Trade

In the decades immediately preceding Independence, many entrepreneurs frequently complained how uneconomic it was to use African slaves, and blamed the high prices brought about by the system of customs duties. For their part, the commercial companies involved in the trade regularly became bankrupt and replaced each other in rapid succession.

---

[5] Sánchez-Albornoz and Moreno, 1968.

[6] This is the author's opinion. Another view can be found in Rosenblat, 1954. The term mestizo has been used in the above context as a total derived from the caste categories mentioned in the previous chapter rather than in a specifically social or cultural sense. For this point consult Borah, 1954.

Without doubt the trade was no longer as lucrative around 1800 as it had been a century before. Nonetheless, the same producers who so bitterly complained of slave labor as uneconomic rigorously opposed the antislavery measures of the new republics of Latin America. Despite the existence of a paid labor force, there were sectors that still needed slaves. The truth is that had it not been for significant events occurring outside the colonies and far removed from their regional necessities, the slave trade would have survived much longer.

The institution of slavery and the trade to which it gave rise had always had, from Fray Bartolomé de las Casas on, its opponents and even bitter enemies. One of the most noteworthy was the Jesuit, Fray Alonso de Sandoval, who at the beginning of the seventeenth century disputed the legitimacy of slavery, and condemned the way the slave traders made up their cargoes—opinions heartily supported by many members of religious orders at the time.[7] Pope Urban VIII, in a bull dated 22 April 1639, condemned the slave trade, seeing it as a means of depriving men of their liberty. In the period around 1689, there were many missionaries preaching in Africa against slavery and the slave trade; and in 1741 Pope Benedict XIV repeated the concepts of the bull of 1639.[8] The eighteenth century was particularly rich in antislave literature and in proposals aimed at improving the legal conditions and actual circumstances of people of Negro blood in America. In Brazil the Jesuits Giovanni Antonio Andreoni and Jorge Benci were especially active. However, the fact that Andreoni had to write under a pseudonym and that later writers on the theme remained anonymous is indicative of the hostility accorded to antislavery books and pamphlets in a society profiting from slavery.[9] Furthermore, these writings had a limited circulation, being known by only an insignificant proportion of the colonial population. It seems highly unlikely, then, that this intellectual opposition had much influence in the long and

[7] Sandoval, 1956. See also the Introduction on this topic and on Sandoval.
[8] Saco, 1937-44.
[9] See, for example, Boxer, 1963.

difficult process of emancipation that was to develop in the following century.

The ideals of human liberty and the critical attitudes toward slavery expressed by the European writers of the Enlightenment produced a similar literature in the Spanish colonies. A group of Jesuits in New Spain are a good example. Around 1780, Francisco Javier Clavijero, as Andrés Cavo had done some years previously, praised the qualities of the mestizos, including those of Negro blood. Another outstanding humanist of the time, the Jesuit Francisco Javier Alegre, in his condemnation of the slave trade, had words of enthusiastic approval for the rebellious attitude and victory of a group of cimarrones who in 1609 had risen in revolt in the region of Orizaba.[10]

The abolition of the slave trade by Great Britain in all its possessions in 1807 was a fundamental step, which had an effect on the various juntas formed at the beginning of the struggle for independence in Spanish America. Abolition of the trade was declared by the Supreme Junta of Caracas in 1810, by Hidalgo in Mexico in the same year, by the Chilean Congress in 1811, and by the government of Buenos Aires in 1812.[11] In 1811 it was even brought up as a motion by the Mexican representative to the constituent assembly

---

[10] Clavijero, 1917; Cavo, 1836; and Méndez Plancarte, 1962. For Orizaba (Mexico), see map 2.

[11] Miguel Hidalgo y Costilla (1753-1811) was the priest whose rebellion (1810) is considered the first open action against the Spaniards which led to the eventual independence of Mexico.

For the abolition of the trade and emancipation of the slaves, consult the following: Good general works are King, 1944b, and Sales de Bohigas, 1970. For Brazil, see Hill, 1931; Adams, 1925; P. A. Martin, 1933; Goulart, 1949; Nabuco, 1949; Graham, 1966; Toplin, 1969; and Bethell, 1970. For Chile, consult *Sesiones de los Cuerpos Legislativos de la República de Chile, 1811 a 1845*, 1887-1908, vols. I and II; Bravo Hayley, 1917; and Feliú Cruz, 1942. Martínez Durán and Contreras, 1962, have studied the theme for Central America. Colombia has Zuleta, 1915; Posada and Restrepo Canal, 1933-38; Bierck, 1953; Hernández de Alba, 1952; and Jaramillo Uribe, 1969. For Cuba, see Corwin, 1967; and Barnet, 1968. For Ecuador, see Bierck, 1953; Peñaherrera de Costales and Costales Samaniego, 1959; and Martínez, 1962. Mexico has been covered by Aguirre Beltrán, 1943; and González Navarro, 1970. Nabuco, 1949, and Pastore, 1949 have dealt with the theme in Paraguay. For Peru, consult *Colección de Leyes, Decretos y Ordenes publicados en el Perú (1821-1830)*, 1831; and Tavara, 1855. For Puerto Rico, see Díaz Soler, 1953; and for Uruguay, Petit Muñoz, Narancio and Traibel Nelcis, 1948; and Carvalho-Neto, 1965. For Venezuela, consult Landaeta Rosales, 1895; Bierck, 1953; and Lombardi, 1967 and 1969a.

which gathered in Cádiz, Spain.[12] It was debated and attacked, and the new Spanish constitution promulgated by the assembly in 1812 made no mention at all of slavery. Great Britain, which perhaps had been the most important power engaged in the trade in the preceding decades, was henceforth the most interested in its abolition and brought as much pressure as it could to bear on those nations that still traded in slaves. The early Latin American juntas had already taken an antislavery stance, and Spain, entering into the same general tendency, then signed a treaty with Britain in 1817 agreeing to abolish the trade in 1820.

The dilatory position of Spain and Portugal toward abolition had been manifest in 1815 at the Congress of Vienna. Here the antislavery declaration made by the nations attending the Congress contrasted sharply with the written declaration made by the representative of the king of Spain who opposed emphatically any foreign intervention in the matter. The Spanish attitude is partly explained by the adamant opposition of many of those concerned with the trade, particularly the representatives of the Cuban planters who in 1810, 1822, and 1823 petitioned against any possible Spanish involvement in a drastic antislave policy. Spain could not afford to ignore what remained of its former empire in what was an especially difficult international situation. In 1835, Great Britain insisted on, and obtained, a new treaty for abolition of the trade, together with stipulations imposing heavy fines and punishments for infringements. This treaty was reinforced by a papal bull on 3 November 1839, which, besides condemning the principles and practice of the trade, imposed excommunication on any Roman Catholic ecclesiastic or layman who engaged in it.[13] However, in spite of all this, the African slave trade continued to Spain's remaining colonies until 1880 (see page 135 below). The Spanish Cortes or parliament had passed a definitive law of abolition nine years before, in 1871.

[12] The famous Cortes de Cádiz, the first constituent assembly in Spain's history, was convoked because of the Peninsular War (for the Spaniards the War of Independence, largely one of popular and guerrilla resistance against Napoleon, 1808-14). The Cortes was essentially an attempt to seek constitutional guarantees against absolute monarchy and create new political structures. Much of the reforming vigor was in fact contributed by the New World spokesmen.

[13] Saco, 1937-44; and Díaz Soler, 1953.

For Brazil, abolition was no less difficult or complex than it had been for the last of Spain's American colonies. Portugal and Britain signed treaties in 1815 and 1817 which, had they been implemented, would have gradually reduced the trade until it eventually disappeared, since they stipulated that slave ships other than those belonging to the signatories were to be seized, and that laws of abolition were to be enacted. The independence of Brazil in 1822 greatly helped the process. Britain, which in a certain sense guaranteed the newly formed Empire of Brazil, was from then on in a position to initiate a protracted series of negotiations and diplomatic moves to gain its objectives. A new treaty was signed in 1826. This fixed a limit of a further three years for the legal operation of the trade, and reaffirmed the provisions of the agreements of 1815 and 1817. But in fact, these early measures availed very little. The opening up of a world market in coffee brought about an unprecedented demand for slaves. From 1820 to 1830 the number of slaves imported legally and illegally increased, remaining for many years at an annual average of 60,000. Legislation enacted in 1830 and 1831, which granted freedom to all illegally imported slaves, specified severe penalties for the smugglers and offered rewards for anyone who helped in exposing them. However, these laws likewise had little notable effect.

British diplomatic representatives and other officials meanwhile kept a close watch for vessels with slaves ("passengers" in many contemporary documents) from Africa, and constantly denounced breaches of the provisions of the treaties to British and Brazilian authorities. Such breaches were so frequent as to be almost the norm. The presence and intervention of British warships near Brazilian coasts eventually created growing strain in the diplomatic relations between the two countries. This was precisely the situation which slave holding interests very much wanted and even actively encouraged. A crisis was reached when the British Parliament unilaterally passed a law in 1845 which not only provided for the continued search of ships suspected of carrying slaves but enpowered Admiralty courts to judge cases of violations of the treaty of 1826. And in April 1850 it was announced that British warships would enter Brazilian territorial waters to apprehend suspected slave vessels. Finally, in September 1850, Brazil promulgated a law to the effect that the slave trade was to be considered and treated as piracy—a move that eventually caused the trade to diminish considerably. The British repealed their law of intervention in Brazilian territorial waters in 1869.[14]

Besides antislave movements, treaties, and international declarations, there were other pressures which were bringing about the decline of African slavery. Paradoxically, such pressures were basically colonialist in nature, but in Africa rather than in America. No colonial possession can develop without an abundant native or imported population. But the establishment of a large slave population seems always to have been accompanied by uprooting and enforced migrations of native peoples, tending to their annihilation, which is what occurred in the Canary Islands, the Antilles, and other parts of America. In a sense Spain learned a lesson by preventing in the New World the type of slavery of local peoples that had developed in the medieval period during the Reconquest of Spain from the Moors, and in the Canary Islands.[15] In its American colonies the enslavement of the native population was more or less normal in the initial years. But toward the middle of the sixteenth century, before the end of the actual period of the conquest itself, the Spanish crown managed to limit enslavement of natives to marginal areas or to regions where the conquest was still active. The economic and social function of the native slaves was replaced by African slaves. But clearly this was bound to have effects of a demographic nature in Africa. Here, initially European domination was by means of coastal trading settlements which mainly depended on the export of slaves. However, at the end of the eighteenth century the European powers who operated the trade started to penetrate into the interior, developing a colonial economy in its own right in much the same way as Spain had done three centuries earlier. They then had to eliminate the slave trade precisely in order to better establish their new economies. Thus it was the growth of colonialism in the African context that came to

[14] See the works cited under Brazil in n. 11 above.
[15] See chap. 1, nn. 3 and 6.

be a major contributing factor in the abolition of the trade and the institution of slavery.[16]

Emancipation Finally Comes

Despite provisions which stipulated freedom from birth for the offspring of slaves, and the antislave declarations issued by the new republics during the early stages of Independence, a relatively active slave trade continued, both in the new republics and in what remained of the old Spanish empire. The Cuban historian, José Antonio Saco, has written a vivid description of what this trade was like during much of the nineteenth century. The clandestine trade which followed legal abolition became highly lucrative because of no taxes or price control.[17] It was carried out with vessels flying the flags of the new republics, frequently with the complicity of their governments. Apart from Brazil, the two great centers of this commerce were the same as they had been during the colonial period: the Caribbean, particularly Cuba and Santo Domingo, and the Plata region.[18]

As a result, Great Britain, which was still the leader in curbing the trade, initiated a long series of diplomatic moves with each of the major Spanish American republics. With the temporary support of Brazil, it circulated instructions in 1835 to its diplomatic agents in Mexico, Venezuela, Colombia, Peru, Argentina, Uruguay, and Chile with the object of persuading these countries to sign treaties against the slave trade. These were signed separately with each country, and in general they repeated the clauses of the treaty which had been drawn up with Brazil in 1826. Essentially they declared the slave trade to constitute piracy, and to be dealt with as such. They prohibited the use of licenses or flags of the signatory nations for any activity connected with the slave trade. Facilities were established to intercept and pursue

---

[16] On this, see Verlinden, 1958a. Great Britain abolished slavery in the British West Indies in 1833. France did the same in her West Indies possessions in 1848.

[17] Saco, 1937-44, vol. II.

[18] King, 1944a. Some documentary material has been published on these themes, and also a number of contemporary narratives. Among others is Captain Canot's very exciting account (Canot, 1854), of his years as a contraband slave runner in the region of the Caribbean.

suspected vessels or smugglers, sometimes including marine patrols.[19] Britain had to use all it diplomatic skills and even political and economic pressures in order to get these treaties signed and ratified. It had, in short, to come to an understanding with local caudillos who were often engaged in disputes over leadership and command in the new republics, and to become involved in disputes concerning boundaries, or to enter into other international agreements and guarantees.

Smuggling of slaves in the Plata region could only be eliminated after negotiation in 1839 with the tyrant Rosas, followed by the ratification of an agreement in 1840.[20] In the same year Uruguay agreed to a treaty which was duly ratified in 1842. Mexico definitively abolished slavery in 1829, but it was not until 1842 that its treaty pledging collaboration with Britain against the clandestine slave trade was signed. The delay was due to a long series of complications with France and with Britain's recognition of the independence of Texas.[21] Venezuela decreed manumission in 1821, but around 1837 there were still almost 38,000 slaves in the country. A treaty was finally signed in 1839 after some difficulties, since the agreement could have caused financial loss and could also have harmed Venezuela's foreign trade. Colombia had a similar number of slaves, in spite of having carefully tried to regulate manumission. For some years during the decade of 1830-1840 there existed a small local slave trade between Colombia and Ecuador which was sufficient to delay either country signing agreements with Britain. Ecuador eventually signed in 1847, and Colombia in 1851.[22]

Negotiations with Bolivia, Peru, and Chile were complicated by the Chilean war against the Peruvian-Bolivian Confederation.[23] After the war the planters on the Peruvian coast initiated a movement for the retention of slavery. The

[19] See the works cited in n. 11 above.

[20] Juan Manuel de Rosas, who had come to power in the anarchy of the years after Independence, first as governor of Buenos Aires (1829) and subsequently as virtual dictator of a confederation of Argentine provinces (1835-52).

[21] See n. 11 above.

[22] See under Colombia, Ecuador, and Venezuela in n. 11.

[23] The Peruvian-Bolivian Confederation was established (1835-36) by Santa Cruz, president of Bolivia, and opposed by Chile, which declared war in 1836 and defeated the Confederation at Yungay in 1839.

result was that Agustín Gamarra signed a law which annulled the antislave decree of San Martín promulgated in 1821. In the end, Peru was persuaded to include an article condemning the trade in a commercial treaty signed with Britain in 1850. Final abolition came in 1854 as a result of the political struggles between President José Rufino Echeñique and Marshal Ramón Castilla.[24] Chile considered that it had no real problem with slavery, at least after 1823, when it freed the 4,000 Negro slaves remaining in the country. Not wanting to contract obligations to deal with a nonexistent problem, and being at war with the Peruvian-Bolivian Confederation, Chile delayed signing a treaty with Britain until 1841.[25]

The legal abolition of slavery in Puerto Rico came in 1873, and in Cuba in 1880. In both countries, the political situation in Spain was an important determining factor. The proclamation of the Spanish Constitution of 1869, and the Cortes of 1882 and 1889 involved strong liberal and even radical groups who had taken up abolition as one of their political objectives.[26] There were other important related questions at the time. Production statistics for the overseas Spanish provinces showed an increase in production as the number of slaves imported diminished, and also as the slaves who were there obtained conditional manumission through the so-called preparatory laws of abolition, which compensated owners by the ex-slaves' continued labor for them.[27] Circumstances were propitious, and Great Britain, this time supported by the United States, made a last, decisive effort. Slavery was abolished without compensation for the owners in Puerto Rico. But the situation was different in Cuba, where six years after abolition was declared, there were some 30,000

[24] See n. 11. It was in the civil strife following on the death of Gamarra (after he had attempted as president of Peru to invade Bolivia in 1841) that Ramón Castilla eventually emerged as president (1845-51). He overthrew Echeñique and again became chief executive or virtual dictator (1855-62).

[25] See n. 11.

[26] The 1869 Constitution came as a result of the September Revolution (1868) against Isabel II, and her subsequent departure from Spain; her position as monarch had long been deteriorating. The Cortes of 1882 and 1889 represented periods of government by the liberal Sagasta, whose coalitions relied on a large variety of groups, radical and otherwise (abolitionists, free-traders, anticlericals, a group known as the Dynastic Left, Catholics, and protectionists.)

[27] Díaz Soler, 1953; and Corwin, 1967.

Negroes working off compensation to their masters; that is, they were still in a state of obligatory semi-slavery with freedom for them far from being clear. This situation was changed by a law enacted in 1886, which gave them their freedom without any conditions whatsoever.

The final process of freedom was no less complex in Brazil. The declaration of 1850 making the slave trade illegal did not signify freedom for the hundreds of thousands of Negroes already in the country, nor did it mean the suspension of clandestine trade. The latter, as might be expected, increased notably. What is more, the demand for coffee and for raw products in a rapidly industrializing world was creating pressures for more labor, providing an even better market for the slave smugglers and creating a much greater demand for paid workers. Such changes soon began to cause changes in Brazilian society. In various cities the population increased almost explosively. A new class of entrepreneurs began to make innovations in techniques of production, while at the same time tending to take on a type of worker for industrial purposes who had not been alienated by long experience of slavery.[28] Especially after 1870, there was a new social environment, with a developed, powerful public opinion and more dynamic and active political ideologies, which supported a militant and effective antislave movement. The resistance of the Negroes on the plantations and their escapes and revolts had the sympathy and backing of the more modern urban society.

Many other elements were propitious for emancipation. One of these was the war waged by Brazil as part of the Triple Alliance against Paraguay (1865-1870).[29] A large number of Negroes gained their liberty by enrolling in the army, and after the war many of them stayed on in the noncommissioned ranks. As a result, the army too became involved with the antislavery campaign and began to refuse to take action against rebel slaves. This meant that the plantation owners were deprived of one of their principal supports in the maintenance of security and compulsory work. In 1887 the

[28] P. A. Martin, 1933; Cardoso, 1962; and Graham, 1966.
[29] The Paraguayan War. The alliance was of Brazil, Uruguay, and Argentina. It was disastrous for Paraguay, especially in the decimation of its population.

army officially petitioned to be excluded from any action against slaves.[30]

Great Britain continued its antislave campaign, using all the political and even economic means at its disposal. Thus the Brazilian emperor, Pedro II, was virtually obliged to refer to the problem of slavery in his annual speech in 1887, as an evil that had to be eradicated. A law giving freedom from birth had been passed in 1871, but in fact it was partly annulled by making such freedom conditional upon obligatory work and economic compensation up to the age of twenty-one. In spite of this, however, it helped to prepare the ground for full abolition. The main factors were the increasing internal and external pressures against slavery, the "inefficiency" of the army in quelling revolts in the plantation regions, and the support given by the urban and new industrial centers to both freed slaves and those on the run. In the decade following 1870 even the most obstinate planters were beginning to think that slavery was becoming no longer worthwhile in view of its increasing danger and low economic productivity. There followed a chaotic and violent period, during which some of the states, like Ceará in 1884, proclaimed complete liberty for slaves in an effort to avoid internal problems. Unfortunately, such measures meant greater difficulties with other provinces having different systems of production and with the large cities, which were increasingly centers of refuge and redistribution of labor. The law of unconditional abolition, when it was eventually proclaimed in 1888, was a measure which had long been desired and awaited by a large part of the population.[31]

At the turn of the present century, the institution of slavery as such was no longer recognized as legitimate in the countries of America. The complete suppression of the trade itself, and then the moves to obtain the unconditional freedom of slaves were a long, difficult, and complex process, making it quite clear how important and deeply rooted the institution had been in Latin America. In each of the countries, and in Latin America as a whole, abolition meant more than merely the legal liberty of a large part of its population.

[30] Graham, 1966; and Toplin, 1969.
[31] Hill, 1931; and Graham, 1966.

Perhaps it is no coincidence that the two countries which delayed the longest suffered fundamental changes shortly afterwards: Cuba ceased to be part of the Spanish Empire in 1898, and Brazil declared itself a republic in 1889.

Substitutes for Slavery

Previous discussion has made clear that slavery was a system of production vital to a certain stage of colonialism as it developed in Latin America, given certain basic demographic circumstances and market demands. Manifest also is the fact that in various situations and places it had begun to be unproductive. An account of the abolition of the trade and the emancipation of the slaves would be incomplete if examined solely from the point of view of legislation against slavery. Also relevant are the alternative methods adopted in place of legal slavery in economic activities that had been hitherto so dependent on it. Slave-holding interests not only opposed antislavery laws and provisions but also sought ways and means of either recreating or prolonging the circumstances characteristic of slavery. They did this by creating categories of workers who under the law were not slaves but who resembled slaves in many basic aspects. There were two main categories: one arose through attempts to either retain as or convert back into slaves many Negroes recently granted their freedom; the other meant enslaving under false pretenses persons who had not before been regarded by tradition or by local and international labor markets as a potential source for servile manpower. Such people were never formally known as slaves; legally they were paid workers. Thus their condition of semi-slavery was a de facto situation created within certain ambits of production.[32] Both these major groups had in common, of course, the fact that their bondage

---

[32] The important qualifying clause here is a "de facto situation created *within certain ambits of production*," since people traditionally considered as slaves were in their places of origin also slaves as a result of de facto situations (tribal warfare, raids, etc.). Nobody in Latin America, from the sixteenth century on, was particularly bothered about the origin of or manner by which the people they were buying had become slaves. The usual phrase stamped on the bills of sale drawn up before the notaries public for recently arrived Africans was "taken in just war," which in fact was no more than a mere formula to complete the legal aspect of a commercial transaction.

was not the result of a commerce in black slaves such as had been traditionally practiced.

Most of the ways of converting ex-slaves, whether they were called liberated, emancipated, or enfranchised, back into slaves were known from the sixteenth century. They had become more widely used and perfected whenever slaves were in especially short supply in some particular area where their use could be highly profitable. Nearly all the ways used have already been mentioned. Here they will be summarized and clarified. Basically there were four: the tracking down and recapture of cimarrones and runaway slaves; the reutilization of freed slaves; obligatory work by way of compensation for liberty sometime in the future; and the breeding of slaves. The capture of cimarrones became the object of extensive legislation, as has been pointed out, from the sixteenth century onward; and it became revitalized and further developed in the last years of the eighteenth century and the early years of the nineteenth. Fugitive slave hunting gave rise to special police forces in all the major cities and also to the formation of armed expeditions and permanent army corps. In the nineteenth century newspapers were extensively used for organizing large sweeps or raids to capture such slaves, to announce escapes and offer rewards, or to gather together owners of runaway slaves so as to arrange ways and means of recapture. New developments were the frequent use of national armies, and the common inclusion, among the recaptured, of white and Oriental workers who had disappeared from their places of work while owing money or before having completed the periods stipulated in their contracts.

The reutilization of freed slaves usually arose in circumstances where international treaties and laws of manumission created considerable numbers of ex-slaves who were legally free but who had to wait to be actually placed at liberty or repatriated to their places of origin. Especially in Brazil and Cuba, officials charged with putting manumission into effect tried to delay it as long as possible, renting out the ex-slaves under contract to plantations or manufacturing establishments. The latter resembled jails more than they did factories. Frequently the ex-slaves were grouped with recaptured cimarrones and sent to other provinces or countries instead of being repatriated or set free in the regions where they had been slaves. Examples are the trade which occurred between Ecuador and Peru, and also between Ecuador and Colombia.[33]

Another type of utilization of the labor of freed slaves occurred in those countries which delayed abolition as long as possible: economic compensation by way of unpaid work had to be made to the owners before liberty was finally granted. The periods of time varied from five to twenty years. Usually these cases were backed by provisions in the laws of manumission, but occasionally other proposals were put forward which were basically similar in attempting to keep freed slaves compulsorily within the plantations, although as paid workers. Such proposals, for example, were presented to the legislative bodies of Brazil, Cuba, and Peru and justified on the grounds of the shortage of labor and decline of production that would result from any exodus of ex-slaves. These economic considerations were quite apart from other social concerns of the upper classes such as an increase in the vices and idleness of the working class.[34]

As the slave trade began to suffer severe setbacks, making it virtually impossible to obtain slaves and then only at very high prices, other more or less long-term projects started, to make alternative supplies available by breeding slaves near some of the major points where they were needed. There was only one known example of this in Latin America before the nineteenth century, at Córdoba, in Argentina, in the middle of the eighteenth century. This region had an active commerce in mules and other agricultural products with the mines of Potosí. The Jesuits bred slaves in one of the haciendas of the area, though it is not clear whether these slaves were intended to form part of the slave trade that operated up through the country to Potosí or whether they were to be employed in some of the other Jesuit agricultural undertakings. The latter alternative seems the more likely, given

[33] Moreno Fraginals, 1964; and Stein, 1970. For Peru, see for example, *El Peruano*, Segundo Semestre, no. 16, 1843.
[34] There is ample evidence of this in the countries mentioned. Consult, for example, the Bibliography under the Peruvian paper *El Conciliador*.

the specific interest that the Jesuits had in training slaves with specialized knowledge and abilities for their particular needs and systems of production.[35] By the middle of the nineteenth century, slave breeding became common in Brazil and Cuba. In Cuba it existed at the very least in Bocaranao and Cienfuegos, being cynically praised by the royal consulado of the island in 1854 as a well-conceived "system of conservation and reproduction."[36] However, various difficulties seem to have prevented breeding from becoming very important. There was of course a great shortage of Negro women of the right age, since female slaves had always been in a lesser number, and also because for some time they had been most usefully employed in various ways in the sugar mills. These circumstances, together with a very high infant mortality, made the slaves produced by breeding very expensive and too few to be able ever to partially replace imported slaves.

The second major group of workers involved in an attempted substitution for legal slavery were those who had always been officially regarded as free. They had accepted and signed work contracts which stipulated extremely low rates of pay, and which offered such other things as the possibility to migrate, liberty after the expiration of the contract period (varying between five and fifteen years), medical care, and the possibility of returning to place of origin, etc. However, in practice these contracts amounted to an endeavor to establish an inflow of workers which essentially was very little different from the importation of African slaves, and which in some cases, as for example that of Indians from Yucatán or the Chinese, was even more cruel and infamous. There were a number of ways in which this new trade was organized: enforced levies of free people, Indian slaves, and immigration from African colonies, Europe, or the Far East. The rounding up of free people and pressing them into service under some legal pretext was far from being new in the nineteenth century. By the end of the sixteenth century there were large numbers of free

---

[35] Concolorcorvo, 1942.
[36] Quoted by Moreno Fraginals, 1964. See also Stein, 1970.

Indians, mestizos, and ex-slaves in the major Spanish American urban centers who were not specifically integrated into either the social structure or the economic life of the time. In other words, there existed a large floating population which in due course would come to replace slavery. Whenever a shortage of labor, an upsurge in the number of vagabonds or of cimarrones, or a temporary suspension of the slave trade occurred for some reason or another, these groups in the cities would be compulsorily recruited under the control of some business proprietor or entrepreneur. It was the cabildos and the magistrates who organized, and who often were the parties who benefited the most from, this type of obligatory work. It was a situation which became especially common in the eighteenth and nineteenth centuries throughout Spanish America, the more so when the effects of uneconomic slavery and the laws of manumission began to be felt. Then many of the freed slaves were prosecuted as idlers and vagrants, with the result that they were sent to work in strongly guarded workshops and factories, together with some whites and every type of mestizo.

The enslavement of Indians was likewise not only confined to the nineteenth century but was a common feature of the sixteenth and seventeenth centuries in both the Spanish and Portuguese possessions of the New World. It had a resurgence as an alternative to Negro slavery at a time when there was a strong universal movement against slavery, and when on the other hand the new republics had reaffirmed that the Indians had rights equal to those of any citizen. The enslavement of Indians never reached major proportions, if one considers the numbers transported, but it was especially used in Cuba with Indian slaves from Yucatán. The first slaves were brought over and sold in the middle of the nineteenth century. A few years later a well-known Cuban slave trader, Francisco Martí Torrens, began trade on a large scale. Each Indian sold for 40 pesos, when a contract for a term of five years for a Chinese worker cost 70 pesos in 1847 and 300 in 1860. The reason for the comparatively lower price for the Indians was largely their low productivity owing to their not being particularly successful at mastering the more technical jobs in the sugar mills, their continual attempts at escape and suicide, and a high mortality rate at young ages. It is impossible to estimate the total number of slaves imported from Yucatán. Small shipments continued to arrive up to 1870. The census of 1862, in which it is obvious that there was an enormous underregistration of all sectors of the population but especially of the slaves, shows only 786 of these Indians working on the island. The concern of the Mexican government and the intervention of the British navy put an end to this trade after 1870.[37]

As all these ways of replacing African slaves, in combination, proved far from sufficient, and as legal slavery tended more and more to disappear, almost incredible proposals were put forward by various parties. Around the mid-century these included plans to bring entire provinces into active production. The projects became particularly popular, for obvious reasons, among the planters. A multitude of projects to import colonists directly from Africa under special work contracts appeared simultaneously in Peru, Brazil and Cuba in the decade after 1840. These proposals were made quite seriously. To convince the public and the national governments of their good intentions, private banks, entrepreneurs and landowners used all the means at their disposal including pamphlets and articles in newspapers and magazines. Legal proposals and petitions with carefully worked-out plans were presented to the goverments, but, as far as is known, no definitive venture or project along these lines ever got under way.[38] Certainly, not all ideas of colonization and immigration were linked with an attempt to replace slave labor. Most of the new republics had quite legitimate desires to colonize regions of scarce population, and especially so when they formed part of the boundary disputes, or had been isolated from the traditional seats of colonial administration. However, such legitimate aims were undeniably useful in demonstrating the good intentions of all projects of colonization. The promoters of immigration were thus divided into two major groups: those who preferred white migrants already trained or with the aptitude for learning new techniques of production, and those who only wanted workers in numbers and little else. It was manifestly the latter group which

[37] Moreno Fraginals, 1964; and González Navarro, 1970.
[38] *Recursos y documentos que manifiestan la necesidad que hay de traer al país colonos africanos* (Lima), 1870. See also E. Romero, 1949.

favored the idea of African colonists, and Asiatic and even European workers, provided there were long contracts, which of course merely amounted to another form of enslavement.[39] Such contracts, for example, were written for some of the Europeans who came to the Caribbean in the first half of the nineteenth century. The first came to Cuba just before 1840 from Ireland and the Canary Islands. Their contracts were for varying periods between one and five years at the extremely low rate of nine pesos a month. In Cuba itself at the time many mulattoes and free Negroes received between 15 and 20 pesos a month. Around 1840 more came from Catalonia and in 1854 others from Galicia, the latter causing serious disturbances in the island shortly after their arrival.[40]

At least in Cuba, by 1850 the attempt to use white labor to replace dwindling Negro slave labor was considered to have failed. This failure was largely brought about by the adamant opposition of the African slave traders, who were still making money out of the trade, and the further opposition of the various governments concerned toward the emigration of workers at a time when the Industrial Revolution in Europe was reaching a new and decisive stage of development. An added factor was that the whites so imported came to a society which was strongly segregationist, and they tended to identify themselves with the white upper classes, so that it was difficult to keep them under the vigilance and control of a semi-slave system. Most of them soon found their way into the new industries and small commerce, leaving the plantations.[41] The only alternative for the planters was to look to India and Asia for labor. As I noted earlier, from the end of the sixteenth century there had existed a small trade in Latin America of so-called Chinese slaves: most of them were in fact Filipinos. This trade was the result of the commercial contacts between the viceroyalties of Peru and New Spain and the Far East by way of the Pacific. By 1807, there were in Brazil serious proposals to import

---

[39] For Brazil at least, the case seems to have been well clarified by Cardoso, 1962.

[40] *El Peruano*, Segundo Semestre, no. 20, 1848. Consult also Moreno Fraginals, 1964.

[41] Moreno Fraginals, 1964.

workers from Asia and India,[42] but eventually such importation became particularly associated with Cuba and Peru, and came to involve especially the Chinese.

The first shipment of Chinese laborers under a work contract arrived in Cuba in 1847 and in Peru in 1854.[43] The terms of contract were usually for periods of five or six years. The salary was minimal. It soon became very lucrative to resell the original contracts, which fetched twice or three times their cost. The demand for Chinese workers was always very high, partly because of their scarcity and partly because they turned out to be extremely good workers, able to work up to 18 hours a day. In addition they were very able, and readily learned new production techniques. Despite their advantages, the treatment given to them was in general no better, if not worse, than that of the Negro slaves of the seventeenth and eighteenth centuries. The Cuban code of 1854 was specifically written with the Chinese and the Indian colonists from Yucatán in mind, but the differences from the laws which applied to the treatment of slaves were virtually nil.

The contribution of the Chinese to the plantation regions of Latin America was very important. Although in Peru their importation began to decline around the middle of the 1870s, an estimated 84,247 Chinese workers entered the country between 1850 and 1874. The figures were much higher in Cuba, where their importation was continued until the present century.[44] Leaving aside statistics and what they represent in the way of a labor force, the significance of the Chinese workers in Latin America is that they proved in the particular historical situation of the time to be the only possible means of transition between the final, remaining systems of slave labor and that of the paid worker. It is the paid worker exclusively who has come to be recognized as the agent of production in twentieth century Latin America.

[42] J. H. Rodrigues, 1965; and Viotti da Costa, 1966.

[43] Stewart, 1951; Moreno Fraginals, 1964; Gutiérrez Seco, 1965; and Segall, 1968.

[44] Stewart, 1951. An interesting point arises here in respect to Cuba. In the first thirty years of the twentieth century a total of 1,082,546 immigrants entered Cuba from Europe, the Antilles, and elsewhere, among whom were at least 60,000 Chinese. This means that Cuba received more workers in the thirty years indicated than all the slaves imported into it during the entire colonial period. See Sánchez-Albornoz and Moreno, 1968.

BIBLIOGRAPHY

1. *Manuscript Sources*

Archivo General de Indias
        Audiencia de Charcas, 32-35
        Audienicia de Lima, Legajo 1095

Archivo Histórico del Cuzco
  Coleción Notarial del Cuzco, siglo XVI
  Registros de:
        Gregorio Vitorero, 1561-1562 (miscellaneous books)
        Antonio Sánchez, 1568 (miscellaneous books)

Archivo Nacional de Colombia
  Sección Colonial. Caciques e Indios. Vols. 4, 33, 47

Archivo Nacional del Perú
  1. Notarios de Lima
  Registros de:
        Pedro de Castañeda, 1537-1538 (miscellaneous books)
        Pedro Salinas, 1538-1540 (miscellaneous books)
        Pedro Gutiérrez, Julio-Agosto, 1544 (miscellaneous books)
        Simón de Alzate, 1548-1551 (miscellaneous books)
        Francisco de Acuña, Vol. XX
  2. Sección Histórica. Esclavos. Legajo 1
  3. Tribunal del Consulado. Legajo 10, Cuaderno 137

Archivo Nacional de Santiago de Chile
  1. Colección Fondo Antiguo. Vol. 24, Pieza 4
  2. Colección Gay-Morla. Vol. 120
  3. Colección Notarios de Santiago
        Vol. 1, 2, 3, 7, 8, 9, 10, 11, 12, 18a, 19, 20, 21, 22, 25, 26, 27,
        28, 31, 32, 36, 46, 52, 53, 54, 80, 83, 100
  4. Colección Real Audiencia. Vols. 45, 88, 131, 187, 316

Biblioteca Municipal de Lima
  Cedulario del Cabildo. Vols. I, III, V, VIII, IX, XIII, XXVI

Bibliography

Biblioteca Nacional de Lima

Sección Manuscritos: C456, C1014, C1033, C1460, D177, D9634

2. *Printed Sources and Reprints*

Actas da Câmara da Vila de São Paulo. 1914-15. 6 vols. Arquivo Municipal de São Paulo.

Andrade e Silva, José Justino de. 1854-57. *Coleção Cronológica de Legislação Portuguêsa.* 10 vols. Lisbon.

Anuncibay, Lic. Francisco de. 1963. "Informe sobre la población indígena de la Gobernación de Popayán y sobre la necesidad de importar negros para la explotación de sus minas." *Anuario Colombiano de Historia Social y de la Cultura* (Universidad Nacional de Colombia, Bogotá), vol. I, no. 1.

Apolant, Juan Alejandro. 1968. *Padrones olvidados de Montevideo del siglo XVIII.* Montevideo.

Arcila Farías, Eduardo (ed.). 1957. *El Real Consulado de Caracas.* Caracas: Instituto de Estudios Hispanoamericanos.

Bravo de Lagunas y Castilla, Pedro José. 1955. *Voto consultivo que ofrece al Excmo. Sr. D. Joseph Manso de Velasco, Conde de Superunda.* Lima.

Calvo, Carlos. 1862. *Colección completa de los tratados, convenciones, capitulaciones, armisticios y otros actos diplomáticos de todos los Estados de la América Latina.* Paris.

Canot, Captain Theodore (pseud. for Théophile Conneau). 1854. *Twenty Years of an African Slaver, Being an Account of His Career and Adventures on the Coast, in the Interior, on Shipboard, and in the West Indies.* Written down by Brantz Mayer. New York.

Castillo, Francisco del. 1925. "Un inédito valioso—Autobiografía." *Revista del Archivo Nacional del Perú,* vol. III.

Cavo, Andrés. 1836. *Los tres siglos de México.* 3 vols. Mexico City.

Clavijero, Francisco Javier. 1917. *Historia Antigua de México.* 2 vols. Mexico City.

Código Criminal do Império do Brasil. 1830. Rio de Janeiro.

Código Filipino ou ordenações e leis do Reino de Portugal. 1869-70. Cândido Mendes de Almeida (ed.). Compiled by order of the King, Philip I of Portugal. 5 vols. Rio de Janeiro: Tip. do Instituto Filomático.

Colección de documentos inéditos relativos al descubrimiento conquista, y organización de las antiguas posesiones españolas . . . de Indias. 1864-1884. 42 vols. Madrid.

Colección de Leyes, Decretos y Ordenes publicadas en el Perú desde su Independencia en el año de 1821 hasta el 31 de diciembre de 1830. 1831. Vol. I. Lima.

Concolorcorvo (*pseud. for Alonso Carrío de la Vandera*). 1942. El lazarillo de ciegos caminantes desde Buenos Aires hasta Lima, 1773. Traditionally regarded as the work of Calixto Bustamante Carlos Inca. Buenos Aires: Ediciones Argentinas Solar.

Documentos para la historia argentina. 1916. Vol. VII. Buenos Aires.

148

Domínguez Bordona, Jesús (ed.). 1936. *Trujillo del Perú a fines del siglo XVIII. Dibujos y acuarelas que mandó hacer el Obispo D. Baltasar Jaime Martínez Compañón.* Madrid.

El Conciliador. 1830. Lima: Imprenta del Estado, no. 29 (April 17).

El Peruano. 1849-1861. (Segundo Semestre, no. 16, 1843; Segundo Semestre, no. 20, 1848; Segundo Semestre, no. 43, November 21, 1849; Primer Semestre, no. 5, January 23, 1852; Segundo Semestre, no. 19, September 10, and no. 36, November 26, 1859; Primer Semestre, no. 24, March 23, 1861).

Encinas, Diego de. 1945. *Cedulario Indiano.* 4 vols. Madrid.

Eschwege, Wilhelm L. von. 1944. *Pluto Brasiliensis.* 2 vols. São Paulo.

Feijoó, Miguel. 1763. *Relación descriptiva de la ciudad y provincia de Trujillo del Perú.* Madrid.

Friede, Juan. 1955-57. *Documentos inéditos para la historia de Colombia.* Vols. I to VI. Bogotá.

———. 1960. *Gonzalo Jiménez de Quesada a través de documentos históricos.* Vol. I, 1509-1550. Bogotá

Gage, Thomas. 1969. *Thomas Gage's Travels in the New World,* ed. J. Eric S. Thompson. Norman: University of Oklahoma Press.

González de Nájera. 1970. *Desengaño y reparo de la Guerra de Chile,* ed. Rolando Mellafe. Santiago: Editorial Universitaria.

Guamán Poma de Ayala, Felipe. 1936. *Nueva crónica y buen gobierno.* Paris.

Hanke, Lewis. 1943. "Las leyes de Burgos de 1512 y 1513." *Anuario* (Sociedad de Historia Argentina, Buenos Aires), vol. XIV (1942).

Herrera, Antonio de. 1945. *Historia general de los hechos castellanos en las islas y Tierra Firme del Mar Océano.* Buenos Aires.

———. 1864. "Idea de las congregaciones públicas de los negros bozales." *Biblioteca Peruana de la Historia,* vol. III.

Jaimes Freire, Ricardo. 1915. *El Tucumán colonial: Documentos y mapas del Archivo de Indias.* Vol. I. Buenos Aires.

Konetzke, Richard (ed.). 1953-62. *Colección de documentos para la historia de la formación social de Hispanoamérica, 1493-1810.* 3 vols. Madrid.

Las Casas, Bartolomé de. 1951. *Historia de las Indias.* 3 vols. Mexico: Fondo de Cultura Económica.

Lavaysse, J. J. Dauxion. 1967. *Viaje a las islas de Trinidad, Tobago, Margarita y a diversas partes de Venezuela en la América Meridional.* Caracas: Universidad Central de Venezuela.

León Pinelo, Antonio de. 1623. *Memorial al Rey Nuestro Señor don Felipe Cuarto en favor de la villa imperial de Potosí, de la ciudad de La Serena, reyno de Chile ... etc., sobre la licencia y permisión para que entren por aquel puerto esclavos de Guinea.* Madrid.

———. 1624. *Señor. La ciudad de la Trinidad, puerto de Santa María de Buenos Aires, gobernación del reino de la Plata, suplica a V. M. se sirva de concederle permisión para navegar por aquel puerto los frutos de su cosecha a Sevilla, Brasil y Angola, en tres navíos de a cien toneladas, en los cuales pueda volver el retorno en las mercaderías y cosas de que carece.* Madrid.

Levillier, Roberto (ed.). 1915. *Antecedentes de política económica en el Rio de la Plata.* 2 vols. Madrid.

———. 1920. *Gobernación del Tucumán: Papeles de gobernadores del siglo XVI.* 2 vols. Madrid.

———. 1921. *Gobernantes del Perú: Cartas y papeles del siglo XVI.* Vol. II. Madrid.

———. 1929. *Ordenanzas de Francisco de Toledo.* Madrid.

Libros del Cabildo de Lima. 1935, ed. Bertram T. Lee. Vol. I. Lima.

Lohmann Villena, Guillermo. 1941-44. "Indice del Libro Becerro de Escrituras." *Revista del Archivo Nacional del Perú, vols. XIV-XVII.*

Márquez de la Plata, Fernando. 1928. "Documentos relativos a la introducción de esclavos negros en América." *Revista Chilena de Historia y Geografía,* nos. 61, 62, and 63.

Martínez Alcubilla, Marcelo. 1885. *Códigos Antiguos Españoles.* Madrid.

Materiales para el estudio de la cuestión agraria en Venezuela (1800-1830). 1964. Introduction by Dr. Germán Carrera Damas. Caracas: Universidad Central de Venezuela.

Medina, José Toribio. 1889-95. *Colección de documentos inéditos para la historia de Chile.* First Series. 30 vols. Santiago, Chile.

Millares Carlo, A., and J. Mantecón. 1945-46. *Indice y extractos de los protocolos del Archivo de Notarías de México, D. F.* Vols. I and II. Mexico City.

Molinari, Diego Luis. 1939. *La representación de los hacendados de Mariano Moreno: Su ninguna influencia en la vida económica del pais y en los sucesos de Mayo de 1810.* Colección de Textos y Documentos Relativos a la Historia Económica Argentina y Americana. Buenos Aires.

Moreyra Paz-Soldán, Manuel, and Guillermo Céspedes del Castillo (eds.). 1954-55. *Virreinato Peruano: Documentos para su historia. Colección de cartas de virreyes. Conde de Monclova.* Vols. I-III. Lima.

Muro Orejón, Antonio (ed.). 1945. "Las Leyes Neuvas, 1542-1543." *Anuario de Estudios Americanos* (Seville), vol. II.

———. 1957. "Ordenanzas Reales para el buen regimiento y tratamiento de los indios." *Anuario de Estudios Americanos* (Seville), vol. XIX.

Ortiz de Zuñiga, Iñigo. 1920-25. "Visita fecha por mandato de su Magestad ..." *Revista del Archivo Nacional del Perú* (Lima).

Ovalle, Padre Alonso de. 1888. *Histórica relación del Reino de Chile.* 2 vols. Santiago, Chile.

Posada, Eduardo, and Carlos Restrepo Canal. 1933-38. *La esclavitud en Colombia: Leyes de manumisión.* 2 vols. Bogotá.

Recopilación de Leyes de las Indias. 1943. (first published 1680). 3 vols. Madrid.

Recursos y documentos que manifiestan la necesidad que hay de traer al país colonos africanos para levantar la agricultura por este medio conocido, de la postración en que hoy se encuentra y promover el desarrollo de las demás elementos de la riqueza pública ... Supremo Gobierno. 1870. Lima.

Rugendas, Maurice. 1853. *Voyage pittoresque dans le Brésil.* Paris: Engelmann.

Sánchez, Galo (ed.). 1919. *Fueros castellanos de Soria y Alcalá de Henares.* Madrid.

Sánchez Ruano, Julián (ed.). 1870. *Fuero de Salamanca.* Salamanca.
Sandoval, Alonso de, S. J. 1956. *De Instauranda Aethiopum Salute.* Bogotá.
Sesiones de los Cuerpos Legislativos de la República de Chile, 1811 a 1845. 1887-1908. 37 vols. Santiago.
Sluiter, Engel. 1949. "Documents Report on the State of Brazil, 1612." *Hispanic American Historical Review,* vol. XXIX, no. 4.
United States Library of Congress, Division of Manuscripts. 1932 and 1936. *The Harkness Collection in the Library of Congress. Calendar of Manuscripts (vol. I), and Documents (vol. II) Concerning Early Peru.* Washington: U.S. Government Printer.
Ureña, Rafael. 1935. *Fuero de Cuenca.* Madrid.
Ureta, José P. (ed.). 1887-91. *Documentos para la Historia de Cartagena.* 4 vols. Cartagena.
Vásquez de Espinosa, Antonio. 1948. *Compendio y descripción de las Indias Occidentales.* Washington: Smithsonian Institution.
Veitia Linage, Joseph de. 1945. *Norte de la contratación de las Indias Occidentales.* Buenos Aires.

3.   *Contemporary Published Works*

Abreu e Brito, Domingos de. 1931. *Um inquérito á vida administrativa e econômica de Angola e do Brasil.* Preface by Alfredo de Albuquerque Felner. Coimbra: Imprensa de Universidade.
Acosta Saignes, Miguel. 1956. "Vida de negros e indios en las minas de Cocorote, durante el siglo XVI." *Estudios Antropológicos, publicados en homenaje al doctor Manuel Gamio.* Mexico City.
———. 1961a. "La trata de esclavos en Venezuela." *Revista de Historia* (Caracas), no. 6, Año II.
———. 1961b. "Los negros cimarrones en Venezuela." *El Movimiento Emancipador de Hispanoamérica.* Madrid.
———. 1962. *Vida de los esclavos negros en Venezuela.* Caracas: Hesférides.
Adams, J. E. 1925. "The Abolition of the Brazilian Slave Trade." *Journal of Negro History,* vol. X.
Aguirre Beltrán, Gonzalo. 1943. "El factor negro en la independencia de México." *Futuro* (Mexico City), no. 91.
———. 1944. "The Slave Trade in Mexico." *Hispanic American Historical Review,* vol. 24.
———. 1946. *La población negra de México, 1519-1810.* Mexico City.
Amunátegui Solar, Domingo. 1922. "La trata de negros en Chile." *Revista Chilena de Historia y Geografía,* vol. XLIV.
———. 1932. "La trata de negros: Apéndice a la parte primera." *Historia Social de Chile.* Santiago, Chile.
Arango y Parreño, Francisco de. 1952. *Obras de Don Francisco de Arango y Parreño.* 2 vols. Havana: Ministerio de Educación.
Arcaya, Pedro M. 1949. *Insurrección de los negros de la Serranía de Coro.* Caracas.
Arcila Farías, Eduardo. 1950. *Comercio entre Venezuela y México entre los siglos XVII y XVIII,* n.p.
———. 1957. *El régimen de la encomienda en Venezuela.* Seville.
Assadourian, Carlos Sempat. 1965. "El tráfico de esclavos en Córdoba, 1588-1610." *Cuadernos de Historia* (Universidad Nacional de Córdoba), no. XXXII.

Bibliography

————. 1966. "El tráfico de esclavos en Córdoba de Angola a Potosí, siglos XVI-XVII." *Cuadernos de Historia* (Universidad Nacional de Córdoba), no. XXXVI.

Barnet, Miguel. 1968. *Biografía de un cimarrón*. Mexico City: Siglo XXI, Editores S. A.

Bastide, Roger. 1967. *Les Amériques Noires: les civilisations africaines dans le Nouveau Monde*. Paris: Payot.

Bauer, Arnold J. 1967. "Manos de obra esclava y libre en ingenios azucareros mexicanos del siglo XVIII." Paper, Tercer Seminario de Historia de Las Americas: Historia Comparativa de la Esclavitud Negra, Viña del Mar, Chile.

Beltrán, Román. 1944. "Africa en América." *Cuadernos Americanos* (Mexico City), vol. XIV.

Berthe, Jean-Pierre. 1958. "Las minas de oro del Marqués del Valle en Tehuantepec. 1540-1547." *Historia Mexicana* (Mexico City), vol. III, no. 29.

————. 1960. "El cultivo del 'pastel' en Nueva España." *Historia Mexicana* (Mexico City), vol. IX, no. 3.

Bethell, Leslie. 1970. *The Abolition of the Brazilian Slave Trade: Britain, Brazil, and the Slave Question, 1807-1869*. Cambridge: Cambridge University Press.

Bierck, Harold A. Jr. 1953. "The Struggle for Abolition in Gran Colombia." *Hispanic American Historical Review*, vol. 33.

Blake, J. W. 1937. *European Beginnings in West Africa, 1454-1578*. London.

Borah, Woodrow W. 1945. "Silk Culture in Colonial Mexico." *Greater America*, California.

————. 1954. "Race and Class in Mexico." *Pacific Historical Review*, vol. 4.

Borges, Analola. 1962. "Fiesta en Caracas (Octubre 1701)." *Revista de Historia* (Caracas), no. 11, Año III.

Boxer, Charles R. 1948. *Fidalgos in the Far East (1550-1770): Fact and Fancy in the History of Macao*. The Hague.

————. 1952. *Salvador de Sá and the Struggle for Brazil and Angola, 1602-1686*. London.

————. 1957. *The Dutch in Brazil, 1624-1654*. Oxford.

————. 1963. *Race Relations in the Portuguese Colonial Empire, 1415-1825*. Oxford.

————. 1969a. *The Golden Age of Brazil, 1695-1750: Growing pains of a Colonial Society*. Berkeley and Los Angeles: University of California press.

————. 1969b. *Four Centuries of Portuguese Expansion, 1415-1825: A Succinct Survey*. Berkeley and Los Angeles: University of California Press, and Johannesburg: Witwatersrand University Press.

————. 1969c. *The Portuguese Seaborne Empire, 1415-1825*. History of Human Society, gen. ed. J. H. Plumb. London: Hutchinson.

Brady, Robert L. 1968. "The Domestic Slave Trade in Sixteenth Century Mexico." *The Americas*, vol. XXIV, no. 3.

Bravo Hayley, Julio P. 1917. *La abolición de la esclavitud en Chile y su relación con nuestros problemas raciales*. Santiago, Chile.

Brito Figueroa, Federico, 1960. *Insurrecciones de esclavos negros en la Venezuela colonial*. Caracas: Cantábrico.

———. 1961. *La estructura social y demográfica de Venezuela colonial.* Caracas.

Browning, James B. 1930. *Negro Companions of the Spanish Explorers in the New World.* Harvard University Studies in History, no. 11.

Canabrava, Alice Piffer. 1944. *O comércio português no Rio da Prata, 1580-1640.* São Paulo.

Carande, Ramón. 1949. *Carlos V y sus banqueros: La Hacienda Real de Castilla.* Madrid: Sociedad de Estudios y Publicaciones.

Cardoso, Fernando Henrïque. 1962. *Capitalismo e escravidão no Brasil Meridional.* São Paulo: Difusão Européia do Livro.

Cardot, Carlos Felice. 1957. *La rebelión de Andresote.* Bogotá.

———. 1961. *Rebeliones, motines y movimientos de masas en el siglo XVIII venezolano, 1730-1781.* Madrid.

Carmagnani, Marcello. 1963. *El salario minero en Chile colonial: Su desarrollo en una sociedad provincial: El Norte Chico, 1690-1800.* Santiago: Universidad de Chile.

Carneiro, Edison. 1946. *Guerra de los Palmares.* Mexico City.

Carranca y Trujillo, Raúl. 1938. "El estatuto jurídico de los esclavos en las postrimerías de la colonización española." *Revista de Historia de América,* no. 3.

Carreira, A. 1968. "As companhias pombalinas de navegação, comércio e tráfico de escravos entre a costa africana e o nordeste brasileiro." *Boletím Cultural da Guiné Portuguesa,* no. 23.

Carvalho Neto, Paulo de. 1955. *La obra afro-uruguaya de Ildefonso Pereda Valdés.* Montevideo.

———. 1958. "La rúa, una danza dramática de moros y cristianos en el folklore paraguayo." *Miscelánea Paul Rivet—Octogenario Dicata,* vol. II, Mexico.

———. 1962. "Contribución al estudio de los negros paraguayos de Acampamento Loma." *América Latina* (Rio de Janeiro), no. 12, Año V.

———. 1964. "Apuntes críticos sobre algunas fuentes antropológicas Afro-Uruguayas." *Boletín Bibliográfico de las Ciencias del Hombre* (Montevideo), no. 1.

———. 1965. *El Negro Uruguayo (Hasta La abolición).* Quito: Editorial Universitaria.

Céspedes del Castillo, Guillermo. 1947. *Lima y Buenos Aires: Repercusiones económicas y politicas de la creación del Virreinato de la Plata.* Seville.

Cevallos, Pedro Fermín. 1886-89. *Resumen de la historia del Ecuador desde su origen hasta 1845.* 6 vols. Guayaquil: Imprenta de la Nación.

Chaunu, Huguette and Pierre. 1956-59. *Seville et l'Atlantique, 1504-1650.* Vols. VI. (1) and VIII (1). Paris.

Chaunu, Pierre. 1962. "Manille et Macao, face à la conjoncture des XVIe et XVIIe siècles." *Annales* (May-June).

Christelow, Allan. 1942. "Contraband Trade Between Jamaica and the Spanish Main, and the Free Port Act of 1766." *Hispanic American Historical Review,* vol. 22.

Clements, Stella Reisley. 1930. "Deed of Emancipation of a Negro Woman Slave, Dated Mexico, September 14, 1585." *Hispanic American Historical Review,* vol. 10, no. 1.

Conrad, Alfred H., and J. R. Meyers. 1964. *The Economics of Slavery and Other Studies in Economic History.* Chicago.

Conrad, Robert. 1969. "The Contraband Slave Trade to Brazil, 1831-1845." *Hispanic American Historical Review* vol. 49, no. 4.

Conzenius, Edouard. 1928. "Ethnological Notes on the Black Carib (Garif)." *American Anthropologist,* New Series, vol. XXX, no. 2.

Cook, S. F., and Woodrow Borah. 1948. "The Population of Central Mexico in 1548: An Analysis of the 'Suma de visitas de pueblos.' " *Ibero-Americana,* vol. 43, University of California.

————. 1960b. *The Indian Population of Central Mexico, 1531-1610.* Ibero-Americana, vol. 44. Berkeley and Los Angeles: University of California Press.

————. 1971. *Essays in Population History: Mexico and the Caribbean.* Vol. I. Berkeley and Los Angeles: University of California Press.

Cook, S. F., and L. B. Simpson. 1948. *The Population of Central Mexico in the Sixteenth Century.* Berkeley and Los Angeles: University of California Press.

Corbitt, Duvon C. 1942. "Immigration in Cuba." *Hispanic American Historical Review,* vol. 22.

————. 1944. "Saco's History of Negro Slavery." *Hispanic American Historical Review,* vol. 24.

Correira Lopes, Edmundo. 1944. *A escravatura, subsidios para su história.* Lisbon: Agência geral das colónias.

Corro, Octaviano. 1951. *Los cimarrones en Veracruz y la fundación de Amapa.* Mexico City.

Corwin, Arthur. 1967. *Spain and the Abolition of Slavery in Cuba, 1817-1886.* Latin American Monographs, no. 9. Austin: Institute of Latin American Studies, University of Texas.

Crouse, N. M. 1940. *French Pioneers in the West Indies, 1624-1664.* New York.

Curtin, Philip. 1969. *The Atlantic Slave Trade: A Census.* Madison: University of Wisconsin Press.

Dalton, Margarita. 1967. "Los depósitos de los cimarrones en el siglo XIX." *Etnología y Folklore* (Havana), no. 3.

Davidson, D. M. 1966. "Negro Slave Control and Resistance in Colonial Mexico, 1519-1650." *Hispanic American Historical Review,* vol. 46.

Davies, K. G. 1970. *The Royal African Company.* New York: Atheneum.

Davis, David Brion. 1966. *The Problem of Slavery in Western Culture.* Ithaca: Cornell University Press.

Debien, Gabriel. 1955. "As grandes plantações de São Domingo nos últimos anos do século XVIII." *Revista de História* (São Paulo), no. 23, Ano VI.

————. 1960a. *La societé coloniale aux XVIIe et XVIIIe siècles. III. Destinées d'esclaves à la Martinique, 1746-1778.* Dakar.

———— 1960b. "Nouvelles de Saint-Domingue." *Annales Historiques de la Révolution Française,* nos. 2 and 4.

De Branche, G. Debien, L. Dermiguz, R. J. Le Gardeur, R. Massio, and R. Pichard. 1960. "Plantations d'Amerique et papiers de famille, II." *Notes d'Histoire Coloniale,* no. 60.

Deer, Noel. 1949-50. *The History of Sugar.* 2 vols. London.

Díaz Soler, Luis M. 1953. *Historia de la esclavitud negra en Puerto Rico, 1493-1890.* Madrid.

Domínguez Ortiz, Antonio. 1952. "La esclavitud en Castilla durante la Edad Media." *Estudios de Historia Social de España* (Madrid), vol. II.

Dusenberry, William H. 1948. "Discriminatory Aspects of Legislation in Colonial Mexico." *Journal of Negro History*, vol. XXXII, no. 3.

Endrek, Emiliano. 1966. *El mestizaje en Córdoba: Siglos XVIII y principios del XIX*. Córdoba, Argentina.

———. 1967. *El mestizaje en el Tucumán: Siglo XVIII. Demografía Comparada*. Córdoba, Argentina.

Escalante, Aquiles. 1954. "Notas sobre el palenque de San Basilio: Una comunidad negra en Colombia." *Divulgaciones Etnológicas* (Barranquilla), vol. III.

———. 1964. *El negro en Colombia*. Monografías Sociológicas, no. 18. Bogotá: Universidad Nacional de Colombia.

Esquemeling, J. 1923. *The Buccaneers of America*. New York.

Feleú Cruz, Guillermo. 1942. *La abolición de la esclavitud en Chile: Estudio histórico y social*. Santiago, Chile.

Fernandes, Florestan. 1970. *A funcão social da guerra na sociedade Tupinambá*. Editora da Universidade de São Paulo.

———. 1971. *The Negro in Brazilian Society*. New York: Atheneum.

Ferreira, Waldemar. 1964. "A política de proteção e elevação das raças exóticas do Brasil nos séculos XVI e XVIII." *Revista da Faculdade de Direito* (São Paulo), 59:4-78.

Foner, Laura, and Eugene D. Genovese (eds.). 1969. *Slavery in the New World. A Reader in Comparative History*. Englewood Cliffs, N. J.: Prentice-Hall.

Freyre, Gilberto. 1966. *The Masters and the Slaves*. New York.

———. 1970. *Order and Progress*. New York.

Galloway, J. H. 1971. "The Last Years of Slavery on the Sugar Plantations of Northeastern Brazil." *Hispanic American Historical Review*, vol. 51, no. 4.

Gandía, Enrique de. 1958. "La insurrección de los negros en Coro en 1795." *Miscelánea Paul Rivet—Octogenario Dicata*, vol. IV. Mexico City.

Garzón Maceda, Ceferino, and José Walter Dorflinger. 1961. "Esclavos y mulatos en un dominio rural del siglo XVIII en Córdoba: Contribución a la demografía histórica." *Revista de la Universidad Nacional de Córdoba*, Segunda Serie, no. 3, Año II.

Genovese, Eugene D. 1971. *The World the Slaveholders Made: Two Essays in Interpretation*. New York: Vintage Books.

Gibson, Charles. 1964. *The Aztecs Under Spanish Rule*. Stanford: Stanford University Press.

Gold, Robert L. 1969. "Negro Colonization Schemes in Ecuador, 1861-1864." *Phylon*, vol. XXX, no. 3.

González, Elda, and Rolando Mellafe. 1965. "La función de la familia en la historia social de Hispanoamérica colonial." *Anuario del Instituto de Investigaciones Históricas* (Rosario), no. 8.

González, Elda, and María Teresa González de Mellafe. 1967. "Una minoría negra en pueblos de indios de Córdoba a fines del siglo XVIII." Paper, Tercer Seminario de Historia de Las Americas: Historia Comparativa de la Esclavitud Negra. Viña del Mar, Chile.

González Navarro, Moisés. 1970. *Raza y Tierra: La guerra de castas y el henequén*. El Colegio de México.

Goulart, Mauricio. 1949. *Escravidão africana no Brasil: Das origens à extincão do tráfico.* São Paulo: Livraria Martins Editôra.

Graham, Richard. 1966. "Causes for the Abolition of Negro Slavery in Brazil: An Interpretative Essay." *Hispanic American Historical Review*, vol. 46, no. 2.

Guerra Y Sánchez, Ramiro. 1964. *Sugar and Society in the Caribbean: An Economic History of Cuban Agriculture.* New Haven: Yale University Press.

Guillot, Carlos Federico. 1961. *Negros rebeldes y negros cimarrones: perfil afroamericano en la historia del Nuevo Mundo durante el siglo XVI.* Buenos Aires.

Gutiérrez Seco, Yolanda. 1965. "Mestizaje peruano-chino." *Revista Histórica* (Lima), vol. XXVIII.

Hamilton, Earl. 1934. *American Treasure and the Price Revolution in Spain, 1501-1650.* Cambridge, Mass.: Harvard Univeristy Press.

———. 1948. *El florecimiento del capitalismo y otros ensayos de historia económica.* Madrid.

Haring, Clarence H. 1910. *The Buccaneers in the West Indies in the XVII Century.* London.

———. 1939. *El comercio y la navegación entre España y las Indias en la época de los Hapsburgos.* Mexico City.

Harth-Terré, Emilio. 1960. *Informe sobre el descubrimiento de documentos que revelan la trata y comercio de esclavos negros por los indios del común, durante el virreinato.* Lima.

———. 1965. "El mestizaje y la miscegenación en los primeros años de la fundación de Lima." *Revista Histórica* (Lima), vol. XXVIII.

Harth-Terré, Emilio, and Alberto Márquez Abanto. 1960a. "El histórico puente del Apurímac." *Revista del Archivo Nacional del Perú* (Lima), vol. XV, entrega I.

———. 1961a. "El artesano negro en la arquitectura virreinal limeña." *Revista del Archivo Nacional del Perú* (Lima), vo. XXV, entrega II.

———. 1961b. "El esclavo negro en la sociedad indoperuana." *Journal of Inter-American Studies*, vol. III, no. 3.

Helps, Arthur. 1848-52. *The Conquerors of the New World and Their Bondsmen, Being a Narrative of the Principal Events Which Led to Negro Slavery in the West Indies and America.* London.

———. 1855-61. *The Spanish Conquest in America and Its Relations to the History of Slavery and to the Government of Colonies.* 4 vols. London.

Hernández de Alba, Gregorio. 1956. *Libertad de los esclavos en Colombia.* Bogotá.

Herskovits, Melville J. 1958. *The Myth of the Negro Past.* Boston.

Hill, Laurence F. 1931. "The Abolition of the African Slave Trade to Brazil." *Hispanic American Historical Review*, vol. 11.

Hoyos Sancho, Nieves de. 1958. "Una fiesta peninsular arraigada en América: Los moros y cristianos." *Miscelánea Paul Rivet-Octogenario Dicata* (Mexico City), vol. II.

Ianni, Octavio. 1962. *As metamorfoses do escravo.* São Paulo.

Jaimes Berti, Jaime, Marianela Parra Bardi, and Graciela Soriano Martínez. 1962. *La sociedad colonial venezolana a través del testimonio de Depous.* Caracas.

James, C. L. R. 1963. *The Black Jacobins: Toussaint L'Ouverture and the San Domingo Revolution.* New York: Vintage Books.

Jara, Alvaro. 1966. *Tres ensayos sobre minera hispanoamericana.* Santiago.

Jaramillo Uribe, Jaime. 1963. "Esclavos y señores en la sociedad colombiana del siglo XVIII." *Anuario Colombiano de Historia Social y de la Cultura* (Universidad Nacional de Colombia), vol. I, no. 1.

———. 1967. *Mestizaje y diferenciación social en el Nuevo Reino de Granada en la segunda mitad del siglo XVIII.* Bogotá.

———. 1969. "La controversia jurídica y filosófica librada en la Nueva Granada en torno a la liberación de los esclavos." *Anuario Colombiano de Historia Social y de la Cultura* (Universidad Nacional de Colombia), vol. I, no. 4.

Jorrín, Silverio. 1944. "Ensayo crítico sobre Saco," [*J. A. Saco*] *Historia de la esclavitud desde los tiempos más remotos hasta nuestros días,* vol. 5. Havana.

King, James Ferguson. 1942. "Evolution of the Free Slave Trade Principle in Spanish Colonial Administration." *Hispanic American Historical Review,* vol. 22.

———. 1943. "Descriptive Data on Negro Slaves in Spanish Importation and Bills of Sale." *Journal of Negro History,* vol. XXVIII, no. 2.

———. 1944a. "Negro History in Continental Spanish America." *Journal of Negro History* (January).

———. 1944b. "The Latin American Republics and the Suppression of the Slave Trade." *Hispanic American Historical Review,* vol. 24.

———. 1944c. "The Negro in Continental Spanish America: A Select Bibliography." *Hispanic American Historical Review,* vol. 24.

———. 1951. "The Case of José Ponciano de Ayarza, a Document on 'Gracias al Sacar.'" *Hispanic American Historical Review,* vol. 31.

Klein, Herbert S. 1967. *Slavery in the Americas: A Comparative Study of Virginia and Cuba.* Chicago: University of Chicago Press.

———. 1971. "The Internal Slave Trade in Nineteenth Century Brazil: A Study of Slave Importations into Rio de Janeiro in 1852." *Hispanic American Historical Review,* vol. 51, no. 4.

Kossok, Manfred. 1959. *El Virreinato del Rio de la Plata: Su estructura económica-social.* Buenos Aires.

Kunst, J. 1916. "Notes on Negroes in Guatemala during the Seventeenth Century." *Journal of Negro History* (October).

Lahmeyer Lobo, Eulalia María. 1962. *Proceso Administrativo Ibero-Americano.* Rio de Janeiro: Biblioteca de Exército-Editôra.

Landaeta Rosales, Manuel. 1895. *La libertad de los esclavos en Venezuela.* Caracas.

Leal, Ildefonso. 1961. "La aristocracia criolla venezolana y el Código Negrero de 1789." *Revista de Historia* (Caracas), no. 6.

León, Nicolás. 1924. *Las castas del México colonial o Nueva España.* Mexico City.

Levene, Ricardo. 1924-28. *Investigaciones acerca de la historia económica del virreinato de la Plata.* 2 vols. Buenos Aires.

Lockhart, James. 1968. *Spanish Peru, 1532-1560: A Colonial Society.* Madison: University of Wisconsin Press.

Lohmann Villena, Guillermo. 1957. *El corregidor de indios en el Perú bajo los Austrias*. Madrid.

Lombardi, John V. 1966. "Los esclavos negros en las guerras venezolanas de la Independencia." *Cultura Universitaria* (Caracas), vol. XIII, pp. 153-168.

———. 1967. "Los esclavos en la legislación republicana de Venezuela." *Boletín Histórico* (Fundación John Boulton, Caracas), vol. XIII, pp. 43-67.

———. 1969b. "Manumission, Manumisos, and Aprendizaje in Republican Venezuela." *Hispanic American Historical Review*, vol. XLIX, no. 4.

———. 1969b. "Sociedad y esclavos en Venezuela: La era republicana, 1821-1854." *Boletín de la Academia Nacional de la Historia*, 52 (207):514-25.

Love, Edgar F. 1967. "Negro Resistance to Spanish Rule in Colonial Mexico." *Journal of Negro History*, vol. LII, no. 4.

———. 1971. "Marriage Patterns of Persons of African Descent in a Colonial Mexico City Parish." *Hispanic American Historical Review*, vol. 51, no. 1.

MacLachlan, Jean O. 1940. *Trade and Peace with Old Spain, 1667-1750: A Study of the Influence of Commerce on Anglo-Spanish Diplomacy in the First Half of the Eighteenth Century*. Cambridge: Cambridge University Press.

McLean Estenos, Roberto. 1947. *Estudios sobre el negro*. Lima.

———. 1948. *Negros en el Nuevo Mundo*. Lima.

Marín-Tamayo, Fausto. 1960. *La división racial en Puebla de los Angeles bajo el régimen colonial*. Puebla.

Marshall, Leon Carroll. 1931. "The Emergence of the Modern Order," in *Industrial Society*, ed. L. C. Marshall, part I, chap. I. Chicago: University of Chicago Press.

Martin, Gaston. 1931. *L'ère des négriers (1714-1771), d'après des documents inédits*. Paris.

Martin, Norman. 1957. *Los vagabundos en la Nueva España, siglo XVI*. Mexico City: Editorial Jus.

Martin, P. A. 1933. "Slavery and Abolition in Brazil." *Hispanic American Historical Review*, vol. 13.

Martínez, Eduardo N. 1962. "Urbina, libertador de los negros: Colaboración." *Boletín del Instituto Nacional Mejía* (Quito), no. 63.

Martínez Alier, Verena. 1971. "Virginidad y machismo: El honor de la mujer en Cuba en el siglo XIX." *Ruedo Ibérico* (Paris), no. 30.

Martínez Durán, Carlos, and Daniel Contreras. 1962. "La abolición de la esclavitud en Centroamérica." *Journal of Inter-American Studies*, vol. IV, no. 2.

Martínez Montero. 1940-42. "La esclavitud en el Uruguay. Contribución a su estudio histórico-social." *Ministerio de Instrucción Pública. Revista Nacional* (Montevideo), nos. 32, 41, 45, and 57.

Mauro, Frédéric. 1956. *L'Atlantique portugais et les esclaves, 1570-1670*. Lisbon.

Mellafe, Rolando. 1954. *Diego de Almagro y el descubrimiento del Perú*. Santiago, Chile.

———. 1959. *La introducción de la esclavitud negra en Chile: Tráfico y rutas*. Santiago, Chile.

———. 1965a. "Agricultura e historia colonial hispanoamericana." *Nova Americana* (Paris: Mouton), no. 1.

———. 1965b. "Problemas demográficos e historia colonial hispanoamericana." *Nova Americana* (Paris: Mouton), no. 1.

———. 1967. "Consideraciones históricas sobre la visita de Iñigo Ortiz." *Visita de la Provincia de León de Huánuco en 1562*. Huánuco, Peru.

———. 1968. "Frontera agraria: el caso del virreinato peruano en el siglo XVI." *Tierras Nuevas: Expansión territorial y ocupación del suelo en América (Siglos XVI-XIX)*, ed. Alvaro Jara. El Colegio de Mexico.

———. 1972. "Descripción tipológica de los documentos útiles para la demografía histórica existentes en los archivos latinoamericanos." *Celade*, Series D. no. 71.

Mellafe, Rolando, Lucía Poblete, and Inés Manzur. 1967. "El grupo negro en la sociedad urbana de Lima del siglo XVI." Paper, Tercer Seminario de Historia de Las Américas: Historia Comparativa de la Esclavitud Negro. Viña del Mar, Chile.

Méndez Plancarte, Gabriel. (ed.). 1962. *Humanistas del siglo XVIII*. Mexico: Universidad Nacional Autónoma de México.

Mendiburu, Manuel de. 1862. "Ojeada a la esclavitud bajo el régimen colonial." *Revista de Lima*, vol. V.

———. 1874-90. *Diccionario histórico biográfico del Perú*. 8 vols. Lima.

Métraux, Alfred. 1958. *Le voudou haïtien*. Paris: Gallimard. (Translated into English by Hugo Charters, *Voodoo in Haiti*, New York: Oxford University Press, 1959.)

Meza, Néstor. 1941. *La formación de la fortuna nobiliaria y el ritmo de la conquista*. Santiago, Chile.

Mintz, Sidney W. 1958. "Historical Sociology of the Jamaican Church-Founded Free Village System." *De West Indische Gids*, vol. 38.

———. 1959. "Labor and Sugar in Puerto Rico and in Jamaica." *Comparative Studies in Society and History*, vol. I. no. 3.

———. 1960a. *The Origins of the Jamaican Internal Marketing System*. New Haven: Yale University Press.

———. 1960b. *Worker in the Cane, a Puerto Rican Life History*. New Haven: Yale University Press.

Miranda, José. 1944. *Notas sobre la introducción de la mesta en la Nueva España*. Mexico City.

———. 1952. *El tributo indígena en la Nueva España durante el siglo XVI*. Mexico City.

Molinari, Diego Luis. 1916. "Data para el estudio de la trata de los negros en el Rio de la Plata." *Documentos para la historia Argentina* (Buenos Aires), vol. VII.

Moreno Fraginals, Manuel. 1964. *El Ingenio: El complejo económico social cubano de azúcar*, vol. I (1760-1860). Havana: National Cuban Commission of UNESCO.

Moreno Toscano, Alejandra. 1968. *Geografía económica de Mexico (Siglo XVI)*. Mexico City: El Colegio de México.

Moreyra Paz-Soldan, Manuel. 1944. *Estudios sobre el tráfico marítimo en la época colonial*. Lima.

———. 1948. *La toma de Portobelo por el almirante Vernon y sus consecuencias económicas*. Lima.

Mörner, Magnus. 1956. "The Theory and Practice of Racial Segregation in Colonial Spanish America." *Proceedings of the Thirty-Second International Congress of Americanists.* Copenhagen.

——. 1966. "The History of Race Relations in Latin America: Some Comments on the State of Research." *Latin American Research Review*, vols. I, III.

——. 1967. *Race Mixture in the History of Latin America.* Boston: Little, Brown.

——. 1970a. *La Corona española y los foraneos en los pueblos de indios de América.* Stockholm: Institute of Ibero-American Studies.

—— (ed.). 1970b. *Race and Class in Latin America.* New York: Columbia University Press.

Murdock, George Peter. 1959. *Africa: Its Peoples and Their Cultural History.* New York: McGraw-Hill.

Nabuco, Joaquim. 1949. *O Abolicionismo.* São Paulo.

Neilson, G. H. 1945. "Contraband Trade Under the Asiento, 1730-1739." *American Historical Review*, vol. LI.

Newton, Arthur Percival. 1933. *The European Nations in the West Indies, 1493-1688.* London: A. and C. Black.

Nina Rodrigues, Raimundo. 1935a. *Os africanos no Brasil.* Revised, with a preface by Homero Pires. São Paulo: Editora Nacional.

——. 1935b. *O animismo fetichista dos negros bahianos.* São Paulo.

Ortiz, Fernando. 1947. *Cuban Counterpoint: Tobacco and Sugar.* New York: Alfred A. Knopf.

——. 1951. *Los bailes y el teatro de los negros en el folklore de Cuba.* Havana.

Ots Capdequí, José María. 1946a. *Nuevos aspectos del siglo XVIII español en América.* Bogotá.

——. 1946b. *El estado español en las Indias.* Mexico City.

——. 1958. *Las instituciones del Nuevo Reino de Granada al tiempo de la Independencia.* Madrid.

Pastor Benítez, Justo. 1955. *Formación social del pueblo paraguayo.* Buenos Aires.

Pastore, Carlos. 1949. *La lucha por la tierra en el Paraguay: Proceso histórico y legislativo.* Montevideo.

Peñaherrera de Costales, Piedad, and Alfredo Costales Samaniego. 1959. "Coangue o historia cultural y social de los negros de Chota y Salinas: Investigación y elaboración." *Llacta* (Quito), vols. IV and VII.

Pereda Valdés, Ildefonso. 1937. *El negro rioplatense y otros ensayos.* Montevideo.

——. 1938. *Línea de color (ensayos afro-americanos).* Santiago, Chile.

——. 1940. "Negros esclavos, pardos libres y negros libres en Uruguay." *Estudios afro-cubanos* (Havana), vol. IV, nos. 1-4.

——. 1941. *Negros esclavos y negros libres: Esquema de una sociedad esclavista y aporte del negro en nuestra formación nacional.* Montevideo.

Pérez de Barradas, J. 1948. *Los mestizos de América.* Madrid.

Pérez de la Riva, Francisco. 1946. "El negro y la tierra: El conuco y el palenque." *Revista Bimestre Cubano*, no. 58.

Pérez de Tudela Bueso, Juan. 1955. "Política de poblamiento y política de contratación de las Indias, 1502-1505." *Revista de Indias* (Madrid), vol. XV.

Pérez Embid, Florentino. 1948. *Los descubrimientos en el Atlántico y la rivalidad castellano-portuguesa hasta el Tratado de Tordesillas*. Madrid.

Petit Muñoz, Eugenio, Edmundo Narancio, and José M. Traibel Nelcis. 1948. *La condición jurídica, social, económica y política de los negros durante el coloniaje en la Banda Oriental*, vol. I, part I. Montevideo: Biblioteca de Publicaciones Oficiales de la Facultad de Derecho y Ciencias Sociales, Universidad de Montevideo.

Pierson, Donald. 1942. *Negroes in Brazil: A Study of Race Contact at Bahia*. Chicago: University of Chicago Press.

Ponce, Fernando. 1967. "Empresa y esclavitud en el complejo económico Jesuita." Paper, Tercer Seminario de Historia de Las Américas: Historia Comparativa de la Esclavitud Negra. Viña del Mar, Chile.

Prado, Caio, Junior. 1971. *The Colonial Background of Modern Brazil*. Berkeley and Los Angeles: University of California Press.

Prado y Ugarteche, J. 1894. *Estado social del Perú durante la dominación española*. Lima.

Querol y Roso, Luis. 1935. "Negros y mulatos de Nueva España: Historia de su alzamiento en México en 1612." *Anales de la Universidad de Valencia*, cuaderno 90, año XII.

Ramos, Arthur. 1943. *Las culturas negras en el Nuevo Mundo*. Mexico City. (Spanish translation of his *As Culturas Negras no Novo Mundo*, São Paulo: Companhia Editora Nacional, 1937.)

Ramos, Demetrio. 1970. *Minería y comercio interprovincial en Hispanoamérica: Siglos XVI, XVII y XVIII*. Universidad de Valladolid.

Ramsay, G. D. 1957. *English Overseas Trade During the Centuries of Emergence*. London.

Revista del Archivo Nacional del Peru, 1920-   . Lima.

Ricard, Robert. 1955. *Etudes sur l'histoire des Portugais au Maroc*. Coimbra.

Riva Palacio, Vicente. 1887-1889. *México a través de los siglos*. 5 vols. Mexico City: Balleseá y Cia.

Rippy, J. Fred. 1921. "The Negro and the Spanish Pioneers in the New World." *Journal of Negro History* (April).

Rodrigues, José Honório. 1965. "Brasil e extremo oriente." *Política Externa Independiente* (Rio de Janeiro), no. 2, ano. 1.

Rodríguez, Mario. 1956. "The Genesis of Economic Attitudes in the Río de la Plata." *Hispanic American Historical Review*, vol. 36.

Rodríguez Molas, Ricardo. 1961. "Negros libres rioplatenses." *Buenos Aires, Revista de Humanidades* (Buenos Aires), no. 1, año I.

Rojas Gómez, Roberto. 1922. "La esclavitud en Colombia." *Boletín de Historia y Antigüedades* (May).

Romero, Carlos A. 1905. *Negros y caballos*. Lima.

Romero, Emilio. 1949. *Historia económica del Perú*. Buenos Aires.

Romero, Fernando. 1939a. "La corriente de la trata negrera en Chile." *Sphinx* (Lima).

———. 1939b. "El negro en Tierra Firme durante el siglo XVI." *Actas y trabajos científicos del XXVII Congreso Internacional de Americanistas*. Lima.

———. 1944. "The Slave Trade and Negro in South America." *Hispanic American Historical Review*, vol. 24.

———. 1965. "El mestizaje negroide en la democracia del Perú." *Revista Histórica* (Lima), vol. XXVIII.

161

Bibliography

Roncal, Joaquín. 1944. "The Negro Race in Mexico." *Hispanic American Historical Review*, vol. 24.

Rosenblat, Angel. 1954. *La población indígena y el mestizaje en América.* 2 vols. Buenos Aires.

Rossi, Vicente. 1926. *Cosas de negros. Los orígenes del tango y otros aportes al folklore rioplatense: Rectificaciones históricas.* Río de la Plata (Córdoba).

Saco, José Antonio. 1859. *Colección de papeles científicos, históricos, políticos y de otros ramos sobre la isla de Cuba.* 4 vols. Paris: Impr. de d'Aubusson y Kugelmann.

———. 1928. *Contra la anexión,* ed. Fernando Ortiz. 2 vols. Havana: Cultural, S.A.

———. 1937-44. *Historia de la esclavitud desde los tiempos más remotos hasta nuestros días.* Vols. IV and V. Havana.

Sales de Bohigas, Nunia. 1970. "Esclavos y reclutas en Sudamérica, 1816-1826." *Revista de Historia de América,* no. 70.

Salmoral, Manuel Lucena. 1962. "Levantamiento de esclavos en Remedios." *Boletín Cultural Bibliográfico* (Bogotá), vol. 5, no. 9.

Sampaio Garcia, Rosendo. 1957. "O português Duarte Lopes e o comércio espanhol de escravos negros." *Revista de História* (São Paulo), no. 30, ano VIII.

Sánchez-Albornoz, Nicolás, and José Luis Moreno. 1968. *La población de América Latina: Bosquejo Histórico.* Buenos Aires.

Sauer, Carl Ortwin. 1966. *The Early Spanish Main.* Berkeley and Los Angeles: University of California Press.

Scelle, Georges. 1906. *La traite négrière aux Indes de Castille: contrats et traités d'assiento.* 2 vols. Paris: L. Larose et L. Tenin.

Scheuss de Studer, Elena Fanny. 1958. *La trata de negros en el Río de la Plata durante el siglo XVIII.* Buenos Aires: Universidad de Buenos Aires.

Schurz, William L. 1959. *The Manila Galleon.* New York.

Segall, M. 1968. "Esclavitud y tráfico de culíes en Chile." *Journal of Inter-American Studies,* vol. 10, no. 1.

Simonsen, Robert C. 1937. *História Econômica de Brasil, 1500-1820.* São Paulo: Companhia Editora Nacional.

Simpson, George E. 1941. "Haiti's Social Structure." *American Sociological Review,* vol. 6.

———. 1955. "Political Cultism in West Kingston, Jamaica." *Social and Economic Studies,* vol. 4.

Simpson, Lesley Byrd. 1950. *The Encomienda in New Spain* (3d ed., 1966). Berkeley and Los Angeles: University of California Press.

Sluiter, Engel. 1948. "Dutch-Spanish Rivalry in the Caribbean Area, 1594-1609." *Hispanic American Historical Review,* vol. 28.

Stein, Stanley J. 1970. *Vassouras: A Brazilian Coffee County, 1850-1890.* New York: Atheneum.

Sternberg, Hilgard O'Reilly. 1970. "A Geographer's View of Race and Class in Latin America." *Race and Class in Latin America,* ed. Magnus Mörner. New York: Columbia University Press.

Stewart, Watt. 1951. *Chinese Bondage in Peru: A History of the Chinese Coolie in Peru, 1849-1874.* Durham, N.C.: Duke University Press.

Tannenbaum, Frank. 1946. *Slave and Citizen: The Negro in the Americas.* New York: Vintage Books.

Bibliography

Taunay, Affonso d'Escragnolle. 1939-43. *Historia do cafe no Brasil.* 15 vols. Rio de Janeiro.

———. 1941. "Subsídios a história do tráfico africano no Brasil colonial." *Revista do Instituto Histórico e Geográfico Brasileiro* (Rio de Janeiro), vol. III.

Tavara, Santiago. 1855. *Abolición de la esclavitud en el Perú.* Lima.

Taylor, William B. 1970. "The Foundation of Nuestra Señora de Guadalupe de los Morenos de Amapa." *The Americas,* no. 26.

Thayer Ojeda, Tomás. 1939-1941. *Formación de la sociedad chilena y censo de la población de Chile en los años 1540 y 1565, con datos estadísticos, biográficos, étnicos y demográficos.* 3 vols. Santiago.

Toplin, Robert Brent. 1969. "Upheaval, Violence, and the Abolition of Slavery in Brazil: The Case of São Paulo." *Hispanic American Historical Review,* vol. 49, no. 4.

Torre Revello, José. 1958. "Un contrabandista del siglo XVII en el Rio de la Plata." *Revista de Historia de América* (July).

Ulloa, Modesto. 1963. *La Hacienda Real de Castilla en el reinado de Felipe II.* Rome: Libreria Sforzini, Centro del Libro Español.

Vega, Juan José. 1965. "Manco Inca y los esclavos negros en la compaña de Titu Yupanqui: El negro que llevó un tesoro incaico." *Revista Histórica* (Lima), vol. XXVIII.

Velázquez, María del Carmen. 1953. "La Real Fuerza de San Diego de Acapulco." *Estudios Históricos Americanos* (Mexico City).

Verger, Pierre. 1953. "Influence du Brésil au golfe du Bénin." *Mémoire de l'Ifan* (Dakar), no. 27.

———. 1954. *Dieux d'Afrique: Culte des orishas et voudou a l'ancienne Côte des Esclaves en Afrique et á Bahia.* Paris.

Verlinden, Charles. 1924. "L'esclavage dans le monde iberique médiéval." *Anuario de Historia del Derecho Español* (Madrid), vol. XI.

———. 1942. "Esclaves du Sud-Est et de l'Est européen en Espagne á la fin du Moyen Age." *Revue Historique du Sud-Est Européen* (Bucharest).

———. 1949. "Précédents et parallèles européens de l'esclavage colonial." *Instituto* (Coimbra).

———. 1955. "L'esclavage dans l'Europe médiévale." *Péninsule Ibérique-France,* vol. I. Bruges, Belgium: De Tempel.

———. 1958a. "Navigateurs, marchands, et colons italiens au service de la découverte et de la colonisation portugaise sous Henri le Navigateur." *Le Moyen Age.*

———. 1958b. "Esclavitud medieval en Europa y esclavitud colonial en America." *Revista de la Universidad Nacional de Córdoba* (Homenaje jubilar a monseñor doctor Pablo Cabrera, 1885-1957).

———. 1961. *Formes féodales et domaniales de la colonisation portugais dans la zone atlantique aux XIVe et XVe. siècles et spécialement sous Henri le Navigateur.* Coimbra.

Vial Correa, Gonzalo. 1957. *El africano en el Reino de Chile. Ensayo histórico-jurídico.* Santiago: Universidad Católica de Chile.

Vignols, Leön. 1929. "El asiento francés (1701-1716) y el comercio franco-español ..." *Anuario Histórico del Derecho.*

Villarán, Manuel Vicente. 1964. *Apuntes sobre la realidad social de los indígenas del Perú ante las Leyes de Indias.* Lima.

Viotti da Costa, Emilía. 1966. *Da senzala à colonia.* São Paulo.

von Lippman, Edmund O. 1941-42. *Historia do Açúcar*. Translated by Rodolfo Coutinho. 2 vols. Rio de Janeiro.

Wagley, Charley (ed.). 1952. *Race and Class in Rural Brazil*. UNESCO.

Weinstein, Allen, and Frank Otto Gattel (eds.). 1968. *American Negro Slavery: A Modern Reader*. Oxford University Press.

West, Robert C. 1949. *The Mining Community in Northern Spain: The Parral Mining District*. Ibero-Americana, vol. 30. Berkeley and Los Angeles: University of California Press.

Westin de Cerqueira, Beatriz. 1967. "Um Estudo de escravidão em Ubatuba." *Estudos Históricos* (Faculdade de Filosofia, Ciências e Letras, Marília, São Paolo, Brazil) no. 6.

Williams, Eric. 1964. *Capitalism and Slavery*. London.

————. 1970. *From Columbus to Castro: The History of the Caribbean, 1492-1969*. London: André Deutsch.

Wolf, Eric. 1953. "La formación de la nación: Un ensayo de formulación." *Ciencias Sociales*, vol. IV.

Wolf, Inge. 1964. "Negersklaverei und Negerhandel in Hochperu, 1540-1640." *Ahrbuch für Geschichte vol Staat, Wirtschaft und Gesellschaft Lateinamerikas*, vol. I.

Wolf, John B. 1951. *The Emergence of the Great Powers, 1685-1715*. New York.

Wright, Richard Robert. 1902. "Negro Companions of the Spanish Explorers." *American Anthropologist* (April).

Zavala, Silvio. 1935. *Las instituciones jurídicas en la conquista de América*. Madrid.

————. 1944. *Ensayo sobre la colonización española en América*. Buenos Aires.

————. 1948. *Estudios indianos*. Mexico City.

————. 1958. "Vida social en Hispanoamérica en la época colonial." *Miscelánea Paul Rivet-Octogenario Dicata* (Mexico) Vol. II.

Zelinsky, Wilbur. 1949. "The Historical Geography of the Negro Population of Latin America." *Journal of Negro History*, vol. XXXIV.

Zuleta, Eduardo. 1915. "Movimiento antiesclavista en Antioquia." *Boletín de Historia y Antigüedades* (May).

Zuluaga, Rosa Mercedes. 1970. "La trata de negros en la región Cuyana durante el siglo XVII." *Revista de la Junta de Estudios Históricos de Mendoza* (Mendoza), Segunda Epoca, 1 (6):35-66.

INDEX

Abolition movement: 63, 84, 93, 97-99, 106-107, 128-129, 132-133, 136-137; delays in, 93, 140; and unproductive slavery, 97; economic base of, 127-128, 136-137; and Church, 128-130; and England, 63, 127-138; unconditional, 137

Absolutism, development of, 51

Acclimatization center for colonists, 17-18

African colonies and abolition, 132-133

African culture, survival of, 34, 109, 111

African slave: uses of, 2, 16, 24-26, 29; and Indian population, 16, 26, 102, 103-104; as ally of occupation, 21, 25-26; nonconfiscation of, 24; owners of, 24-25; importation of, 14-19, 24; qualities of, 16, 84; social acceptability of, 26-27; reaction to enslavement, 30, 32-33; numbers of, 72-74; death rate of, 92, 98; in the army, 136

Agricultural economies, 52, 55, 83, 88-93

Alegre, Francisco Javier, humanist, 129

Alliances against Spain, 35

Andean provinces: Indian population in, 17, 30, 31; mining in, 31, 79; supply of slaves, 77, 103

Andreoni, Giovanni Antonio, abolitionist, 128

Angola, 68

Anne, Queen of England, 51

Annuities, slave, 22-25, 42. *See also* Asiento, system of

Antilles: and establishment of slavery, 2, 16-19, 35, 45; occupation of, 30, 36; racial problems in, 104

Arabs, legal heritage of, 10

Arango, Francisco de, abolitionist, 98

Araucanian Indians, 32

Army and abolition, 136-137

Asiento, system of, 44-50, 59-60

Asiento of the Grillos, 48-49

Atahaulpa, 23

Atlantic coast and smuggling, 79

Azores Islands and slave trade, 11, 13

Bad caste, 113-114

Baker, Peter, slave trader, 60, 62

Bankers and slave trading, 39

Bantu, 68

Barbados: British occupation of, 37; and slave trade, 56; distribution center, 65, 79

Barracoons, 69

Barroso del Pozo, Juan, asentista, 49

Barry, Edward, slave trader, 60

Benci, Jorge, abolitionist, 128

slave trade, 57, 98, 99; and slavery, 77, 124; mining in, 87; plantation economy in, 90; slave revolt in, 108; racial composition of, 126; abolition movement in, 134
Violent resistance of slave, 32-33. *See also* Revolution, slave
Visigothic Spain, 10

War of the Spanish Succession, 54
Wars of Independence, 121
Watchmen, slaves as, 87

Welser banking firm and slave trade, 39
West India Company of Amsterdam, 49
White labor, importation of, 143-144
Whitening process, 120. *See also* Integration, racial
Wine production, 89-90
Women in slavery, 117-118

Zambo, 115
Zape, 68
Zuazo, Licentiate, 15, 104-105